THE BOOK OF REVELATION

As It Relates to
Contemporary Christian Living

Taught By

Dr. Ralph Richardson

THE BOOK OF REVELATION As It Relates to
Contemporary Christian Living

Bible Alive Ministries
P.O. Box 2222
Fayetteville, NC 28302

biblealive@juno.com
www.biblealiveministries.org

CatPav Publishing
catpavpublishing@yahoo.com
www.catpavpublishing.com

THE BOOK OF REVELATION
As It Relates to Contemporary Christian Living

Preliminary Remarks on Revelation

As we embark on a verse-by-verse study of this culminating prophecy of the Bible, it is our primary intention to exalt the Lord Jesus Christ and to bring eternal glory to our great Triune God!

We further purpose to provide the challenge and the tools for Christians to engage in daily, disciplined Bible study, without which there is no true spiritual growth in the life of the believer.

Four Applications for Today's Christian

The book of Revelation was not divinely preserved for the Church today simply to excite us regarding prophetic matters (Antichrist, the Tribulation, Armageddon, and the Second Coming). Dr. Merrill C. Tenney suggests four ways in which revelation may be meaningful for us today:

[1] The Interpretation of History – Revelation spans past history as it bears on modern life. A study of this prophecy will confirm that (a) No human empire can endure permanently; and (b) God's concern for His people is the same today as it was in the first century.

[2] Prediction of the Future – Revelation predicts specifics in regards to a one-world government in the end time; the "Beast" (Antichrist) having world-wide authority (13:7); a new world order founded on the redemptive work of Christ; the destruction of this present world; and the creation of new heavens and new earth.

[3] Theological Issues – Revelation contributes in a theological way to the entire structure of Christian thought and doctrine. These truths, such as the doctrines of God, Christ, the Holy Spirit, the Church, the Christian life, and last things, are being challenged today by the false teachings of cults and the occult.

[4] A Source of Spiritual Strength – Revelation confirms God's control over all things and thus serves to encourage and strengthen the daily life of the believer.

The Command **Not** to Seal the Book

In Revelation 22:10 the angel said to John, *"Seal not the words of the prophecy of this book"*. The reason given was *"the time is at hand"*. In God's calendar the time is always at hand (literally, "near"). The Christians of that day, just as you and I today, needed to have an understanding of what God is doing and what he is going to do!

In his commentary on Revelation, Dr. John Walvoord makes this fitting comment: "The time period in which the tremendous consummation of the ages is to take place, according to John's instruction, is near. The indeterminate period assigned to the church is the last dispensation before end-time events and, in John's day as in ours, the end is always impending because of the imminent return of Christ at the rapture with the ordered sequence of events to follow."

"He Who testifieth these things saith, Surely I come quickly. Amen. Even so, come, Lord Jesus." (Revelation 22:20)

A CORRELATION OF DANIEL/REVELATION

Definition of Correlation: 1. The act of showing a causal relationship between two things or two persons. 2. The recognition that two things are so related that one directly implies or is complimentary to the other.

The following quotations support the fact that there is a definite causal relationship, mutually complimentary, between the O.T. Book of Daniel and the N.T. Book of Revelation:

1. In his book, **Daniel: The Key to Prophetic Revelation** Dr. John Walvoord states "In many respects Daniel is the most comprehensive prophetic revelation of the Old Testament, giving the only total view of World history from Babylon to the second advent of Christ and interrelating Gentile history and prophecy with that which concerns Israel. Daniel provides the key to the overall interpretation of prophecy, is a major element in pre-millennialism, and is essential to the interpretation of the book of Revelation."

2. Dr. John Phillips, former professor at Moody Bible Institute, author and Bible teacher, states: "Revelation is closely related to the book of Daniel, to which it forms a sequel". (A subsequent development like the next installment).

3. Quoting the New Scofield Reference Bible, "The Book of Daniel, like the Revelation in the NT is called an **apocalypse** as are Isaiah 24-27 (The Isaiah Apocalypse) and the visions of Zechariah. Apocalypse means unveiling. When wickedness seemed supreme in the world, and evil powers were dominant, an apocalypse was given to show the real situation behind that which was apparent and to indicate the eventual victory of righteousness upon the earth. Apocalyptic writing uses many

figures and symbols. God used this literary form to convey His truth to His people."

Thus, there is a definite correlation between the Books of Daniel and Revelation. Both are so related that one directly implies, or is complimentary to the other. Three of a number of correlations are reviewed below.

      A.   Daniel's prophecies envision the totality of **The Times of the Gentiles** (Luke 21-24), which encompass four vast empires:

1. Babylon
2. Medo-Persia
3. Greece
4. Rome

It is significant that no other world empire has superceded Rome, and Daniel becomes the great key to Revelation, revealing that the Gentile world system, which will ultimately be destroyed by the STONE...cut out without hands (Daniel 2:34-35). Daniel then points us to the fourth and the last Gentile world power...Rome... which becomes the focal point of God's judgment in the Revelation of John.

      B.   In Daniel's Vision of Seventy Weeks (9:24-27) the seventieth week, reference to the 7 year Tribulation, becomes the subject of the greater part of John's Revelation (Chapters 6-18), again mentioning the complementary nature of the two books written some 600 years apart.

      C.   Both books have significant information on the king of fierce countenance (Dan. 8:23) whom we know as the **Anti-Christ** of the Tribulation Period. (Compare Dan. 11:36 with Rev. 13:1-10).

INTRODUCTION TO
THE BOOK OF REVELATION

While speaking of the Bible in general, F.F. Lunsden could well have specified the Book of Revelation when he said:

"Christ is it's grand subject, our good, the design and glory of God, its end. It should fill the memory, rule the heart and guide the feet. Read it slowly, frequently and prayerfully. It is a mine of wealth, a paradise of glory and a river of pleasure. It is given you in life, will be opened at the judgment and be remembered forever. It involves the highest responsibility, will reward the greatest labor and will condemn all who trifle with its sacred contents."

WHO WROTE REVELATION?

The human author calls himself "John" five times (1:1,4,9; 21:2; 22:8), identifying himself as Christ's servant, and a brother and companion in tribulation to those to whom he wrote (1:1-9). There are many similarities between this book and the Gospel of John, as well as 1st, 2nd and 3rd John. The earliest Church Fathers believed, as do we, that John the beloved Apostle wrote the book (Justin Martyr, Iranaeus, Tertullian, Hippolytus, Clement of Alexandria and Origen are among early Christian writers who confirm this.)

TO WHOM WAS REVELATION WRITTEN?

This question may be answered in a twofold way:

1. Historically, we read in 1:4, "John, to the seven churches which are in Asia". Chapters 2 & 3 will reveal the churches.

2. Practically, since "all Scripture is profitable for doctrine, reproof, correction, instruction in righteousness..." we may confirm that the book was written to the Church in general and to every believer in particular.

WHAT WAS THE TIME
AND PLACE OF WRITING?

John, who was overseer of the churches in Asia Minor (western Turkey of today), had been exiled to the Isle of Patmos by Roman Emperor Domitian (1:9); who ruled from A.D. 81 until his death in A.D. 96. It is thought that John was released shortly after Domitian's death, at which time he probably recorded his spirit-revealed revelations. Note 1:9, "I, John ...was in the Isle called Patmos", indicating the actual recording after his exile. Thus, John probably wrote from Ephesus about A.D. 95.

WHY WAS REVELATION WRITTEN?

It is obvious from 1:1-20 that John was inspired to reveal who Jesus Christ is in His glorious Person and what Christ would do in His Sovereign program for the future.

Intending this letter to be a comfort as well as a challenge to faithfulness for followers of Christ, John was given a message with the divine purpose of

[1] Exalting Christ as Head and Lord of the churches (1:4-20);

[2] Correcting the moral and doctrinal problems in the seven churches in Asia Minor (2:1-3:22);

[3] To provide much information on the seven year tribulation period, and the three series of divine judgments to be poured out. (4:1-18:24);

[4] To describe the glorious second advent of Christ to earth with all the attending and subsequent events (19:1-20:1);

[5] To provide a general account of the final judgment on Satan and all unsaved (20:7-15); and

[6] To reveal God's plan for the eternal estate, including the destruction of the present heavens and earth and the creation of new heavens and new earth (21:1 - 22:21)

HOW IS REVELATION STRUCTURED?

God has provided the structure for the book in His statement to John (1:19): *"Write the things which thou hast seen, the things which are, and the things which shall be hereafter."*

Based on this passage, Revelation falls into 3 natural divisions:

Chapter 1   *"the things which thou hast seen"* (past: Vision of Christ)

Chapter 2-3 *"the things, which are"* (present: Vision of the seven churches)

Chapters 4-22 *"the things, which shall be hereafter"* (future: Vision of the future)

HOW DO WE SEE JESUS IN THIS BOOK?

From the very first words, *"The Revelation of Jesus Christ..."* it becomes obvious that the entire book centers in the Person (chap 1) and Program (chpts 2-22) of our great God and Savior, the Lord Jesus Christ! In fact, the last two verses of the final chapter say, *"Even so, come, Lord Jesus. The grace of our Lord Jesus Christ be with you all. Amen."*

THE NAMES AND TITLES OF CHRIST
IN THE BOOK OF REVELATION

1:5   The First Begotten of the Dead
       The Prince of the Kings of the Earth
1:8   The Alpha and Omega
       The Lord Who is...and Was and is to come
       The Almighty
1:13 The Son of Man
1:18 The First and the Last
       The Living One
2:18 The Son of God
3:14 The Amen
       The Faithful and True Witness
       The Beginning of the Creation of God
4:11 The Creator
5:5   The Lion of Judah
       The Root of David
5:6   The Lamb that was Slain
5:9   God
7:17 The Lamb
12:10 The Christ
19:11 The Faithful and True
19:13 The Word of God
19:16 The King of Kings
       The Lord of Lords
22:5 The Lord God
22:13 The Beginning and The End
22:16 The Bright and Morning Star

Is there any question that Jesus is indeed God of gods and Lord of lords?

OUTLINE OF THE
BOOK OF REVELATION
(Based on 1:19, the key verse)

Introduction, 1:1-8
    Source of the Revelation (vs.1-3)
    Salutation from the Revelator (vs. 4-8)

I.   Vision of the Christ, 1:9-20 ("Things which you have seen")
    A. His Pronouncement (1:9-11)
    B. His Portrait (1:12-18)
    C. His Program (1:19-20)

II.   Vision of the Churches, 2:1- 3:22 ("The things which are")
    A. Christ Speaks to the Church at Ephesus (2:1-7)
        1. Who He Is (vs.1)
        2. What He Knows (vs. 2-4)
        3. What He Commands (vs. 5-6)
        4. What He Promises (vs. 7)
    B. Christ Speaks to the Church at Smyrna (2: 8-11)
        1. Who He Is (vs.8)
        2. What He Knows (vs.9)
        3. What He Commands (vs. 10)
        4. What He Promises (vs. 11)
    C. Christ Speaks to the Church at Pergamus (2:12-17)
        1. Who He Is (vs.12)
        2. What He Knows (vs. 13)
        3. What He Commands (vs. 14-16)

a. The Lamb Identified (vs. 5-7)

b. The Lamb Worshipped (vs.8-14)

B. Vision of the Seven Seal Judgments (6:1-8:1)
1. The First Seal: A White Horse (6:1-2)
2. The Second Seal: A Red Horse (6:3-4)
3. The Third Seal: A Black Horse (6:5-6)
4. The Fourth Seal: A Pale Horse (6:7-8)
5. The Fifth Seal: Slain Saints (6:9-11)
6. The Sixth Seal: Ecological and Political Upheaval (6:12-17)
7. The Seventh Seal: Seven Trumpet Judgments (8:1)

First Parenthetic Section (7:1-17)
The Sealed Jews (7:1-8) *The Saved Gentiles (7:9-17)*

``C. Vision of the Seven Trumpet Judgments (8:2-11:19)
1. The First Trumpet: Earth is burned (8:2-7)
   a. Angelic Preparation (vs.2-6)
   b. Divine Devastation (vs. 7)
2. The Second Trumpet: Oceans become blood. (8:8-9)
3. The Third Trumpet: Fresh waters made bitter (8:10-11)
4. The Fourth Trumpet: Day/Night Cycle broken (8:12-13)
5. The Fifth Trumpet: Locust torment the unsaved (9:1-12)
6. The Sixth Trumpet: Four angels and a vast army (9:13-21)

Second Parenthetic Section (10:1-11:14)
(1)The Angel and Little Scroll (10:1-11)
(2)The Measuring of the Temple (11:1-2)
(3)Activities of Two Witnesses (11:3-14)

7. The Seventh Trumpet: The Triumph of Christ (11:15-19)

Third Parenthetic Section (12:1-14:20)

(1) Tribulation Realities: Woman with Child (12:1-2)
(2)Tribulation Realities: The Great Red Dragon (12:3-4)
(3)Tribulation Realities: Male Child (12:5-6)
(4)Tribulation Realities: War in Heaven (12:7-12)
(5)Tribulation Realities: Persecuted Woman (12:13-17)
(6)Tribulation Realities: The Beast Out of the Sea (13:1-10) The Beast out of the Land (13:11-18)
(7)Tribulation Realities: The Lamb and the 144,000 (14:1-5)
(8)Tribulation Realities: Everlasting Gospel (14:6-7)

(9)Tribulation Realities: The Doom of Babylon (14:8)
(101)Tribulation Realities: The Doom of the Worshippers of the Beast (14:9-12)
(11)Blessedness of those who die in Christ (14:13)continued:

14

> *(12)Tribulation Realities:* The Wrath of God
> on the Earth *(14:14-20*

D. Vision of the Seven Bowl Judgments (15:1-16:21)

1. Preparation for the Seven Final Plagues (15:1-8)
2. The First Bowl: Putrefying sores on the un-saved. (16:1-2)
3. The Second Bowl: Death of all sea creatures (16:3)
4. The Third Bowl: Fresh waters become blood (16:4-7)

The Fourth Bowl: Men scorched with fire (16:8-9)

The Fifth Bowl: The Beast's Kingdom turned to darkness (16:10-11)

The Sixth Bowl: Euphrates River dried up (16:12-16)

The Seventh Bowl: History's greatest earthquake (16:17-21)

> ## Fourth Parenthetic Section (17:1-19:10)
> *(1) Destruction of Ecclesiastical   Babylon (17:1-18)*
> *(2) Destruction of Commercial Babylon (18:1-24)*
> *(3) Heavenly Scene of praise to God (19:1-6)*
> *(4) Marriage of the Lamb (19:7-10)*

E. Vision of Christ's Second Coming (19:11-21)
1. Details of His Return (19:11-16)
2. Results of His Return (19:17-21)
    a. The Supper of the Great God (19:17-19)
    b. The Judgment of the Beast and False Prophet (19:20-21)

F. Vision of Final Things (20:1 - 22:5)
1. Satan bound for One Thousand Years (20:1-3)
2. Christ's Millennial Reign (20: 4-6)
3. Satan's Loosing and Doom (20: 7-10)
4. The Great White Throne judgment (20:11-15)
5. The Eternal State of the Redeemed (21:1-22:5)

The Grand Conclusion: (22:16-21)

1. Faithful and True Words (22:6-19)
2. Come, Lord Jesus! (22:20-21)

"Nobody can say exactly in what generation the end will come; but it is obvious that an end must come and that the swiftly passing years are bringing it constantly nearer. Perhaps within the lifespan of many now inhabiting the earth, the Lord may finish the work begun at Calvary. This is the Christian's hope, and the answer to the crowning prayer of the book of Revelation... Amen...Come, Lord Jesus, Come."

Merrill C. Tenney

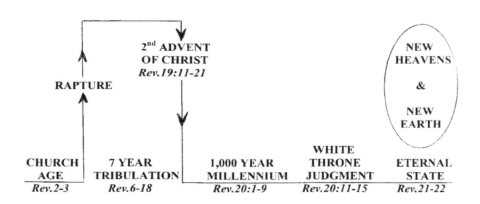

CHURCH AGE	7 YEAR TRIBULATION	1,000 YEAR MILLENNIUM	WHITE THRONE JUDGMENT	ETERNAL STATE
Rev.2-3	*Rev.6-18*	*Rev.20:1-9*	*Rev.20:11-15*	*Rev.21-22*

COMMENTARY ON

THE BOOK OF REVELATION

Introduction, 1:1-8

In a very real sense the first three chapters of this book could be considered introductory, since they are written to the seven churches of Asia (1:11) and reveal the needs that prompted the visions given to the Apostle John. However, since John's first vision begins with verses 9 and 10, the introduction properly comprises only verses 1 through 8.

1. **Source of the Revelation (vs. 1-3)** In these verses we see both the <u>presentation of the source</u> of this book and the <u>promise to the reader.</u>

     a. Presentation of the Source of the Revelation (1-2) *"The Revelation of Jesus Christ, which God gave to Him..."* Take a moment to read these two verses and notice a four-fold source:

- The Father gave the information to Jesus.
- Jesus gave it to His angel.
- The angel gave it to John.
- John bore witness of all that he saw.

First and foremost, whatever other purposes God has for the book; Revelation is a glorious disclosure of the Person and program of Jesus Christ! In fact, Rev.19: 10 declare, *"The testimony of Jesus is the spirit of prophecy"*. That is, the very purpose of all the prophetic scriptures is to testify to (to unveil) the Person and program of our Lord Jesus Christ!

The word **"Revelation"** is *apokalupsis* in the Greek text and means "revealing", "unveiling", that is, "a disclosure of truth concerning divine things before unknown" (Thayer's Greek/English Lexicon of the New Testament).

"...things which must shortly come to pass" does not mean that the events may occur soon (in John's day); but that when they <u>do</u> occur they will be sudden (compare *"the time is at hand"* in verse 3). Thus, these events, when they do come to pass, will happen quickly and suddenly. Such events are revealed in Revelation 6 through 22, beginning with God's wrath in the great 7 year Tribulation, continuing through the Return of Christ to earth, His glorious millennial reign, the destruction of this earth and the heavens, and the creation of New Heavens and New Earth in the eternal state.

b. Promise to the Reader of the Revelation (3)
Dr. Harry Adams, pastor emeritus of Church of the Open Door in Fayetteville makes a fitting statement of this passage: "Prophecy is not just to be heard, but heeded. It should change the way we live. Even so, at the outset of the Book of Revelation, the Apostle John writes:

'Blessed is he who reads and those who hear the words of the prophecy, and <u>heed</u> the things that are written in it' (1:3, NASV)

Prophecy should not only inform us, but also transform us. If after hearing the prophetic message we go about our business as usual, we have not heeded it no matter how well we heard it. As you join in the study of the Book of Revelation, always ask yourself, 'How should my life be different as a result of this study?' If the study of prophecy does not change the way we relate to the world, we have not heeded it, no matter how well we have heard.

2 Salutation from the Revelator (vs. 4-8)

Interestingly, just as there is a four-fold source of revelation in verses 1 & 2, so there are four agents in verses 4 & 5.

a. Affirmation of the Four Agents of the Revelation (4-5a) a careful reading will reveal these to be:

- John the Apostle (4a) *"John"*
- God the Father (4b) *"Him Who Is and Was, and Is to Come."*
- God the Holy Spirit (4c) *"the seven Spirits"* (the perfections of the Holy Spirit – Compare Isaiah 11:2)
- God the Christ *"And from Jesus Christ..."*

b. Explanation of the Person and Program of Jesus Christ (5b-7)

[1] Who He Is

- *"Who is the faithful witness"* That is, His testimony concerning Himself is trustworthy, and what He declares throughout this Book is true! (Read John 7:7 and I Tim. 6:13)
- *"The first begotten of the dead"* As first born from the dead, referring to His bodily resurrection (He is called "the first fruits" in I Cor. 15:20), Christ is the first manifestation of a new kind of life in which all believers shall ultimately share.

20

- *"The Prince (Ruler) of the kings of the earth"* – This is His title as the victorious Conqueror and Establisher of the Kingdom on earth (yet to come).

[2] <u>What He Has Done (5c-6)</u>

- *"Unto Him Who loves us (present tense) and washed us from our sins in His own blood"* **Note**: The only means of cleansing and loosing from the condemnation of sin is Christ's precious blood! (1 Peter 1:18-19)
- *"And has made us a kingdom of priests unto God and His Father, to Him be glory and dominion forever and ever. Amen."* (Compare 1 Peter 2:9)

[3] <u>What He is Going to Do (7)</u>

"Behold, He cometh with clouds, and every eye shall see Him, and they also who pierced Him; and all kindreds of the earth shall wail because of Him. Even so, Amen."

This is a clear reference to Christ's Second Advent to earth, <u>not</u> to His coming for the Church (see chart, page 20). Compare Zech. 12:10; 14:4ff; Matt. 24:29-31; 25:31

c. Declaration of the Alpha and Omega (8) "I am Alpha and Omega, the beginning and the ending, saith the Lord, Who is, and Who was, and Who is to come, the Almighty."

<u>"Alpha and Omega"</u> is referred to 4 times in Scripture (Rev. 1:8, 11; 21:6; 22:13). The emphasis seems to be on the Divine Trinity, Father, Son, and Holy Spirit, though Christ is speaking here.

<u>"The Almighty"</u> = Ruler of all, holding sway over everything and everybody. Jesus Christ, Sovereign Ruler of the universe is the central Figure in these opening verses to Revelation, as well as throughout this powerful prophecy. Here Christ is unveiled as the rightful Ruler of the earth, the King of kings! *"The kingdoms of this world are become the kingdoms of our Lord, and of His Christ: and He shall reign for ever and ever."* (Rev. 11:15)

I. Vision of Christ, 1:9-20 *"The things which you have seen..."*

The present things that were revealed to John include this glorious vision of the Son of Man. But first, John describes his own circumstances.

A. John's Pronouncement (1:9-11)

1. John's Physical Situation (vs. 9)
I John, who also am...

"I John" is used three times in this book (1:9; 21:2; 22:8). Notice that the great apostle (also the last living apostle at the time of writing Revelation) humbly identifies himself with fellow Christians.

a. Your Brother & Companion (vs. 9a)

The word "brother" means literally, "out of the same womb." This speaks of the family bond we all share in Christ (I John 3:2). John lists three things, which he shares with all believers:

(1) *In Tribulation* **– In Jn. 16:33 Jesus said,** *In the world ye shall have tribulation: but be of good cheer; I have overcome the world.* Tribulation here speaks of the undeserved suffering that comes to the child of God because of the enmity of the world and the devil (2 Tim. 3:12; I Thess. 3:3, 4). He describes the reason for his own present trials in the last half of this verse. [John is not referring to the outpouring of God's wrath known as "the great tribulation" since the Church will be raptured (I Thess. 1:10; 4:13-18; Rev. 3:10) prior to God's judgment being poured out on the earth.] *Tribulation* refers to the process of beating the chaff out of the wheat and speaks of our experiential sanctification – God's means of purifying believers for greater usefulness (I Pet. 1:6,7; 4:1). John knew what it meant to suffer. Tradition records that he was thrown into boiling oil and miraculously lived! Now he is imprisoned on a hard-labor island at age 96!

(2) *In the Kingdom* – Like Brier Rabbit, Christians are born and bred in the briar patch. But Halleluiah, the sufferings of this present time are not worthy to be compared to the glory that shall be revealed in us (Rom. 8:18)! In Act 14:22 we read: *exhorting them to continue in the faith...that we must through much tribulation enter into the kingdom of God.* Suffering in time prepares us to rule with Christ in His kingdom (Rom. 8:17; 2 Tim. 2:12; I Pet. 2:21).

(3) *In Patience* – John knew firsthand that *tribulation worketh patience*...literally, "load bearing capacity" or "endurance." Fine flour only results from the process of grinding. Spiritual endurance can come only by means of trials. Instead of complaining when suffering comes our way, we need to praise God (Jam. 1:2-4; 1 Thess. 5:16-19)! If you have allowed bitterness or self-pity to take root in your heart, why not confess it to the Lord Jesus, beloved? Oh, how we need the mind of Christ today.

b. His Prisoner (vs. 9b) *I John...was in the isle of Patmos...*Patmos is a small, rocky outcropping in the Aegean Sea about 15 miles in circumference. It is SW of Ephesus on the coast of modern Turkey. John was banished to this Roman stone quarry by Emperor Domitian. What was John's crime?

(1) *Because of the Word of God* – John's great theme is that "Jesus is Lord." The early Christians were threatened with death for failure to repeat the loyalty oath of Rome, "Caesar is Lord." The day may be coming when you and I will be faced with such life or death decisions. In fact, isn't that what happened to young Cassie Bernall of Columbine High in Colorado?! She said, "Yes!" to Christ and embraced certain death. John said, "Yes!" to Christ and "No!" to Caesar. What will you and I say when put to the test, dear friend?

(2) *Because of the testimony of Jesus Christ* – Jesus is indeed Lord. Proclaiming this truth without apology will place us at odds with the world system (Jn. 15:18). The Roman Empire confined John on Patmos to prevent him from preaching about Jesus Christ, and yet it was on that island that God gave John this revelation of Christ, which has inspired the church for 2,000 years (Rev. 1:1, 2)! Indeed, man's extremity is God's opportunity.

2. John's Spiritual Situation (vs. 10-11)

a. *I was in the Spirit on the Lord's Day* (10a)

The vision of the apocalypse came to John by means of a supernatural, ecstatic experience similar to that of Ezekiel, Peter and Paul (Ezek. 2:2; 3:12-14; Acts 10:10-11; 11:5; 22:17-18).

The Lord's Day probably refers to Sunday, the first day of the week (Mt. 28:1; Mk. 16:2; Lk. 24:1; Jn. 20:9; Acts 20:7; 1 Cor. 16:2), although it may mean that John was transported forward in time to witness the events known in prophetic as "the Day of the Lord" (Isa. 2:12; Joel 1:15; Zech. 14:1; Mal. 4:5; 2 Pet. 3:10). [Three different "days" are revealed in scripture: *The Day of Christ* – the rapture; *The Day of the Lord* – the period beginning with the Great Tribulation and concluding with the final judgment of Satan; and *The Day of God* – which ushers in the New Heaven and Earth.]

b. *I heard a great voice (vs. 10b, 11)*

John is startled by a voice like a war trumpet (cf. Ex. 19:19; Ezek. 3:12). It was Jesus Christ Himself speaking! Trumpets always herald the presence of the King (1 Thess. 4:13f; Rev. 4:1). In verse 11 the eternal Christ (cf. 1:5, 8, 17b, 18) gives instructions *(see, write, send)* to his servant John regarding the seven churches (1:4).

B. Christ's Portrait (1:12-18)

Here we have the only true portrait of Jesus ever painted for the Church, and this picture of our Savior is worth a thousand words! This is how he must have appeared on the mount of transfiguration and how we shall see Him someday (Mt. 17:2; 1Jn. 3:2) in glory.

1. Portrait of Authority (v.12-13)

And I turned...in the midst of the seven candlesticks one like unto the Son of man...

The seven lamp stands represent the seven churches of Asia (vs.20) [believers are to be light-bearers in the world (Mt. 5:14-16)]. Christ is in their midst, evaluating them. Before the Lord reveals to John the extent of His judgment on the unbelieving world, His examination begins with the Church (1 Pet. 4:17). I don't think His ministry of inspection is very popular in the Church today, but it should be (1 Cor. 11:27-32).

"Son of Man" is a familiar title of Christ as Messiah (Dan. 7"13; Mat. 24:30; Acts 7:56) used 84 times in the Gospels.

a. Robe of Divinity (vs. 13a) *...clothed with a garment down to the foot.* This describes the beautiful vestures of our High Priest and King (Isa. 6:1-5). The long flowing robe is symbolic of His authority both to intercede and to judge (Ps 50:4; Heb. 5:5; 9:11-15).

b. Girdle of Authority (vs. 13b) *...girt about the paps with a golden girdle.* One who is busy girds himself about the loins (Isa. 11:5), but he who girds himself about the breast has ceased from his work (Heb. 4:10). Here Jesus is the glorified risen Lord, not the humble servant (Jn. 13:4).

2. Portrait of Purity & Omniscience (vs.14)

a. Head of Purity and Maturity – *His head and His hairs were white like wool, as white as snow...* Proverbs 16:31 says, "A [white head of hair] is a crown of glory." In Daniel 7:9-13, the Ancient of Days is similarly described. White speaks of His absolute purity (Mt. 17:2; Heb. 7:26).

b. Eyes of Omniscient Scrutiny – *His eyes were as a flame of fire.* Christ is here searching out the works of His Church. His penetrating eyes expose everything, cutting through every facade and pretense! Nothing can escape His scrutiny, *Neither is there any creature that is not manifest in His sight: all things are naked and opened unto the eyes of Him with Whom we have to do* (Heb. 4:13; cf. 1Cor. 1:31, 32; 3:11-15; 2 Thess. 1:7-9). We are told in 2 Chron. 16:9, *For the eyes of the Lord run to and fro throughout the whole earth, to shew himself strong in the behalf of them whose heart is perfect toward him* (cf. Jer. 24:6; Amos 9:4; Hab. 1:13). Beloved, what reflection do you see when you look into His eyes? We know what He sees in the Church, because He records it in Chapters 2 & 3.

3. Portrait of Sovereign Omnipotence (v.15-16)

a. Feet of Judgment (v.15a) – *And His feet like unto fine brass, as if they burned in a furnace...*Brass [burnished bronze] is always a symbol of God's judgment against sin (Ex. 27:1-8; Jn 3:14; Dan. 10:6). Placing your foot over the enemy also depicts judgment and triumph (Gen. 3:15; Ps. 110:1; Ps. 60:12).

b. Voice of Power (v.15b) – *and His voice as the sound of many waters.* Psalm 29:3 says, *The voice of the Lord* *is upon the waters: the God of glory thunders: the Lord is upon many waters. The voice of the Lord is powerful; [and] full of majesty.* In Job 40:9 we read, *Have you an arm like God? Or can you thunder with a voice like Him?* What a word picture this is! His voice reverberates like the thunderous roar of Niagara Falls (Ezek. 1:24; 42:2). His voice brought the world into existence and raised the dead...who can resist His power?! We need to listen to His voice (Mt. 17:5; Heb. 3:7).

c. Sword of Sovereignty (v.16a) - *...out of his mouth went a sharp two-edged sword:* The Word of God is the basis for all judgment (Isa. 11:4; Jn. 12:48; 2 Thess. 2:8; Heb. 4:12; Rev. 19:12-15).

d. Face of Sublime Glory (v.16b) – *His countenance was as the sun shineth in his strength.* Christ's appearance was overwhelming to John. We cannot look upon the sun directly without damaging our eyes...so it is with God's Glory (Ex. 33:18-20; Jud. 13:22). Yet, we have beheld His Glory and we shall see His face and live (Gen. 32:30; Jn. 1:14; Rev. 22:4). The hymn writer put it this way:

"Face to face with Christ, my Savior,
Face to face what will it be?
When with rapture I behold Him,
Jesus Christ who died for me!
Face to face I shall behold Him,
Far beyond the starry sky;
Face to face, in all His glory,
I shall see Him by and by!"

Oh, now that will be glory for every child of God!

4. Posture of John (v.17a) – *And when I saw Him, I fell at His feet as dead.* The revelation of glory was too much for John, who falls prostrate before Jesus. So it was with Daniel (8:17), Ezekiel (1:28) and Paul (Acts 9:3-4). Consciousness of our sinfulness and His holiness will keep us humble before God and man!

5. Personal Portrait (v. 17b-18) – *He laid His right hand upon me, saying...Fear not; Christ* gives John a threefold comfort in these verses by presenting himself as:

>   **a.** *I am the first and the last* – the Eternal One (Isa. 41:4; 44:6; 48:12; Rev. 1:11).

>   **b.** *I am he that lives...was dead...alive forever* – The Living God (Jer. 10:10; Jn. 14:6; 1 Tim. 3:15).

>   **c.** *I have the keys of hell and death* – The Authority over death and hell (Rev. 22).

C. Christ's Program (1:19-20)

Christ reveals His divine outline for the book and explains two symbols (stars and lamp stands) in this chapter. *Messengers* refer to the human pastors of each church or to ministering angels assigned duties and responsibilities in the invisible arena (Heb. 1:4).

II. Vision of the Churches, 2:1-3:22   *"The things which are..."*

It is strikingly clear that the letters written by Christ to the seven churches are intended to carry a spiritual message for any era of churches and Christians. In mid-1700 a Lutheran scholar named Johannes Bengel strongly recommended careful meditation on these messages, saying, "Scarcely anything is so fitted to affect and purify us."

Before looking at the passage, it is interesting to note some repeating patterns in these letters:

♦ Each letter gives

[1] The **Church** name.

[2] A description of **Christ**.

[3] A **Commendation** where applicable.

[4] A **Criticism** when necessary.

[5] A **Counsel** to meet the need.

[6] A **Challenge** with promise to those who overcome.

♦ In each letter Christ says *"I know your works"* and *"I will"* (do this or that).

♦ Each letter repeats the call, *"He that hath an ear, let him hear what the Spirit saith to the churches"*.

♦ Each letter repeats the promise, *"To him that overcometh."*

♦ There are four ways to view these seven churches:

[1] **Practically** – As they existed in John's day.

[2] **Perennially** – Conditions that have always existed in local churches.

[3] **Personally** – Conditions true of individual believers.

[4] **Prophetically** – Looking at these churches in a historical perspective, Progressive church history from the Apostolic Age to the Age of Grace (each letter describes dominant characteristics of a particular period of church history). Thus

******

*****

Ephesus – The spiritually powerful Apostolic church from A.D. 32 to 100.

Smyrna – The period of persecution under pagan Roman rulers. A.D. 100-300.

Pergamos –A.D. 300-400, when the church, being united with the state under Constantine, saw a corruption of vitality and testimony.

Thyatira – Spiritual darkness ("dark ages"), including the Reformation, which persists today. A.D. 500-1600.

Sardis – The development and corruption of Protestantism following the Reformation. A.D. 1600 and following.

*Philadelphia - The pure missionary church of the last days, faithful to God's Word and looking for Christ's return. 1900's to the Rapture.

*Laodicea – The corrupt, apostate church of the last days. 1900's to the Rapture.

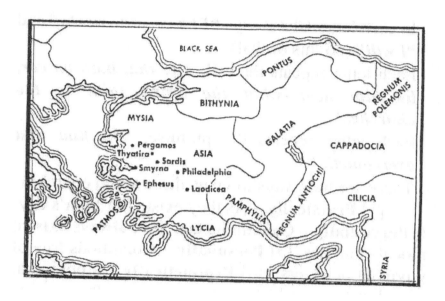

HISTORICAL NOTES ~ EPHESUS

(From *Son of Man Vision*, by Duane Spencer)

Ephesus had one of the great seaports of the ancient world. However, the Cayster River filled it with silt as quickly as it could be dredged. By the sixth century, the war with sand and mud was lost, and with the loss of the harbor, the city died. Today, the ruins of Ephesus are miles from the coast!

Three great Roman highways converged upon this city, making it a center of commerce (especially for the silver-smiths). Ephesus's importance politically was reflected in her title: *"The Supreme Metropolis of Asia."*

She was also a "Free City," which meant that there was no Roman garrison – a rare privilege!

Ephesus was also the center for one of the Seven Wonders of the Ancient World, the Temple of the Greek fertility goddess, Artemis, known to Romans as Diana (cf. Acts 19, where the occult paraphernalia destroyed was equal to the value of a year's wages for 138 men!). The Greeks used to say, *"The sun sees nothing more magnificent in its journey than the Temple of Artemis!"* This pagan temple offered the right of asylum to anyone within 200 yards, regardless of his crime! The people of the city took pride in being the willing slaves of *"The Queen of Heaven."*

Ephesus was the residence of the Apostle John before and after his exile on Patmos. Aquila, Priscilla, Apollos, and Timothy also lived and served there. Ephesus represents the Apostolic Church from A.D. 30-100.

A. Christ Speaks to the Church at Ephesus (2:1-7)

1. Who He Is (vs.1) It is significant that the description of our Lord, different in each letter, fits the need of that particular church.

a. He sovereignly controls and directs the angelic ministry to each church and individual, whether we think of the "stars" (see 1:20) as angelic messengers or as human messengers of each church. *"These things saith he that holds the seven stars in His right Hand..."*

In his commentary on Revelation, Dr. John Walvoord states: "These messengers were probably the pastors of these churches or prophets through whom the message was to be delivered to the congregation."

b. He is continually present among the churches. *"...Who walks in the midst of the seven golden lamp stands."* While this declaration confirms the Deity of Christ (His omnipresence – everywhere present at one and the same time), it also speaks of His protection and control over His own. Isn't it a blessed reassurance that our Lord is always right where the action is taking place! Praise His Name!!!

2. What He Knows (vss.2-4) While verse 1 speaks of Christ's omnipresence, these verses address His omniscience in total knowledge. Hebrews 4:13 says "All things are open and laid bare before Him with Whom we have to do." Notice that He knows both what is desirable in the church and what is detrimental to the church:

a. What is Desirable (2-3) *"I know thy works...?"*

(1) *"labor"* – strenuous, exhausting toil. They were a hard-working church.

(2) *"patience"* - steadfast endurance in the work of the Gospel. (Compare verse 3)

(3) *"cannot bear those who are evil"* – Unlike our day of compromise, they had a holy abhorrence of all that was morally and spiritually bad. Referring to their insistence on exposing false apostles, William R. Newell states, "Ministerial courtesy had no place in Ephesus!"

b. What is Detrimental (4)

"Nevertheless, I have somewhat against you, because you have left your first love." Notice, they had not <u>lost</u> their first love for Christ; rather, they had departed from the fervency and depth of meaning they once had for their Savior. This is indeed the beginning of that decline which, if not corrected, will end in the self-sufficiency of Laodicea ("I have need of nothing", 3:17). What about you? Has your warmth and desire for Jesus degenerated in cold and meaningless religion?

3. What He Commands (vss.5-6)

The command here is to remember, repent, and repeat! They, as you and I must, were to go back to the beginning where their heart burned with love for Christ. At one time, they had been a people of great faith and fervent love (Eph. 1:15), to whom Paul said, "Grace be with all them that love our Lord Jesus Christ in sincerity" (Eph. 6:24).

In <u>verse 6</u> He warns the church that failure to *"repent and do the first works"* would result in being removed from out of their place. While the Ephesus church remained for several centuries, it, along with the city, declined and eventually became uninhabited. Excavations of the city began in 1897 and archaeologists have uncovered about a fourth of Ephesus.

Also, in <u>verse 6</u> is a reference to the hateful *"deeds of the Nicolatians"* (literally, "laity conqueror"). These were a group of people in the church who were exalting clergy over laity. According to early church fathers, such as Ignatius, Clement, and Tertullian, they also promoted dissention and careless living in the church.

4. What He Promises (vs.7*) "He that hath an ear, let him hear what the Spirit saith unto the churches: To him that overcometh will I give to eat of the tree of life, which is in the midst of the paradise of God."* The word for "overcome" is *nikao*, which means "to conquer...to carry off the victory". Positionally, as to our salvation, Christians are always overcomers. Experientially, in our daily walk, we <u>may</u> or <u>may not</u> be overcomers.

The purpose behind the reference to *"the tree of life"* was to rekindle a fervent love for Christ! The tree of life was lost in Genesis 3:22. Those who appropriate "the tree of death", Christ's sacrificial death at Calvary, will regain the tree of life in the eternal Paradise (Rev. 22:2, 14, 19). The promise in verse 7 is related to future rewards for those who are victorious as overcomers who love Jesus fervently.

HISTORICAL NOTES ~ SMYRNA

(From *Son of Man Vision,* by Duane Spencer)

Smyrna (modern Izmir), about 35 miles north of Ephesus, was one of the few planned cities of the world. City coinage bore the inscription, "First in Asia in beauty and size." Its most famous boulevard was the "Avenue of Gold," lined by luxurious, pagan temples and leading to its thriving, safe harbor. Its title as "The Glory of Asia" may have come from the hill called Mount Pajos, adorned with graceful columns and temples, which appeared like a glorious crown above the city as ships entered the port.

Smyrna boasted impressive public monuments (*including a very prominent one erected in honor of her native son, Homer),* a great library, a massive stadium, and the largest open air theatre in all of Asia.

Although not the first city to institute emperor worship, Smyrnans arrogantly boasted that no other province of Rome surpassed its devotion to the worship of Caesar! It was here that Polycarp, beloved bishop of the church of Smyrna, and a disciple of John, was burned at the stake.

The word "smyrna" means "bitter," and is rendered "myrrh" in the New Testament (Mt. 2:11; Mk. 15:23; Jn. 19:39). Smyrna represents the post-apostolic, persecuted church (A.D. 100-313) up to the time of Constantine.

B. Christ Speaks to the Church at Smyrna (2:8-11)

1.   Who He Is (vs. 8) While Ephesus was the church characterized by unwholesome *familiarity,* Smyrna was characterized as a church of *fear.* Under severe persecution, they needed to know that Jesus was *"the first and the last, Who was dead, and is alive."* Just as He died and arose in victory, so death holds no "sting" and the grave no "victory" for those in Christ!

2. What He Knows (vs. 9) It is always reassuring for the suffering saint to realize that God knows every oppression, every pain, and every loss of His child.

"poverty" = Not only lack of resources; they had been robbed of all they possessed! They are reminded, as we must be, that *"you are rich"* – No amount of loss can compare with the wealth of the child of God! Read 2 Cor. 6:10; Jas. 2:5; 1 Pet. 1:6-7.

Of interest is the fact that Smyrna was a very wealthy city, once called "The Ornament of Asia". Today, Smyrna is a large modern city, now called Izmir (over ½ million people).

Included in **what He knows** is *"the blasphemy of them who say they are Jews, but are of the synagogue of Satan."* False religion under satanic control has always been zealous in opposing what is true. 1st century Jews were among the most active enemies of the followers of Christ.

3. What He Commands (vs.10) *"Fear none of those things which you shall suffer...Be faithful unto death..."* Their worst suffering was yet to come, the devil (in control of Gentile and Jewish haters) would cast some of them into prison in his attempts to destroy the Christian influence in his sphere of control.

What is the *"ten days"* of tribulation? Bible scholars have suggested a number of solutions. The probability is that "ten days" signifies a definite, though brief and limited time of persecution, including imprisonment and even death for some. The promise of *"a crown of life"* is synonymous with the promise in verse 11 of not being hurt of the second death. Walvoord states: "Though their own lives might be sacrificed, their real riches were as far removed from this world as the heavens are above the earth...Their crown would be life eternal itself. Indeed, as Paul declares in Romans 8:18, *"The sufferings of this present time are not worthy to be compared with the glory which shall be revealed in us."*

4. What He Promises (vs.11) With no word of rebuke to these precious believers, what Jesus promises through the Spirit is, *"He that overcomes shall not be hurt of the second death."* The "second death" is synonymous with the lake of fire in Revelation 20:11-15. These saints at Smyrna were already overcomers in Christ and would not appear at the White Throne Judgment of the unsaved. They are here assured of eternal blessings in the presence of the Lord Jesus. Commenting on this promise in his book titled Interpreting Revelation, Dr. Merrill C. Tenney states: "The victor will be delivered from the peril of destruction which awaits the wicked." Instead of fear, let us rejoice in God's guarantee of life eternal!

HISTORICAL NOTES ~ PERGAMOS

(From Son of Man Vision, by Duane Spencer)

Pergamos was a capital city ... with a commanding view of both mountain peaks and isles. It was an ancient seat of government for more than 400 years, when in A.D. 30 the first temple to Caesar as a god was erected there. Over 100 years before Christ, the King of Pergamum bequeathed it as a gift to the Roman Empire [who] made it the capital of Asia Minor.

Although it was not the equal of Ephesus and Smyrna commercially ...it was far superior historically. From the stand-point of culture, Pergamos had the honor of possessing one of the finest libraries in the world [second only to that of Alexandria, Egypt], containing over a quarter of a million volumes in a day when all books were copied by hand.

Pergamos had its great pagan temples [also]. High above the city, jutting out from the side of a mountain, was erected the tremendous alter of Zeus Soter ("Zeus, the Savior"). The city acropolis also included the temple of Asklepios, the god of medicine, whose symbol was a staff intertwined by two serpents! Apparently the people of Pergamos were enthusiastic worshippers of serpent-gods since coins, buildings and bas-reliefs in the city prominently displayed serpents.

C. Christ speaks to the Church at Pergamos (2:12-17)

1. Who He Is (vs.12) "Tolerance" is the word that best describes the situation in this church. Its Greek name means "elevation and union." Historically this church represents the period under Constantine when the church was "elevated" from poverty and persecution and was "married" to the political system of Rome (2 Cor. 6:14-16). To this church, and those like it today, Christ describes himself as *He who has the sharp sword with two edges* (1:16; 2:16; 19:15, 21; Eph. 6:17; Heb. 4:12). The sword speaks of pending judgment based upon His absolute truth.

2. What He Knows (vss. 13-15)

a. Commendation (vs. 13)

Our Lord begins His critique with words of affirmation! In spite of the evil influences of pagan idolatry, believers were maintaining their loyalty to the Name of Christ and refused to deny their faith in Him. This apparently led to the death of one called Antipas. We know nothing else about this spiritual hero except Jesus' own description of him as *my faithful martyr* (cf. Phil. 1:21).

Where Satan's throne is...where Satan dwells – may refer to the altars of Zeus and Asklepios, or to Pergamos as the center of Caesar worship. From history we know that as the center of Caesar worship. From history we know that Satan changed his tactics from "a roaring lion" to that of "an angel of light" in the time of Constantine by encouraging tolerance of evil through union with political influence [*from overt attacks to covert corruption*].

b. Criticism (vs. 14, 15) The Lord is grieved with believers in Pergamos for two reasons: tolerance of immorality [Balaam] and false doctrine [Nicolatians]

      (1) *The doctrine of Balaam* is found in Numbers 22-25, where the priest of Midian caused Israel to sin by encouraging fornication and intermarriage with idolaters, thus corrupting true worship. [*The way of Balaam* (2 Pet. 2:15) was becoming a "prophet for hire." *The error of Balaam* (Jude 11) was thinking that he could trick God into cursing Israel because of the nation's sins.] Compromise with the world is a slippery slope leading to sin and deception in which our testimony is lost (1 Cor. 5:1 ff; 10:14-21)!

      (2) *The doctrine of the Nicolatians.*

      According to the early church fathers, the followers of Nicolas advocated loose morals (Rom. 6:1) and promoted a clerical hierarchy [Nicolatians means, "conquering the people"] ~ denying the priesthood of every believer in Christ (1 Pet. 2:9). Jesus' attitude about such teaching is clear..."*which thing I hate.*"

3. What He Commands (vs.16)

      Repent or else I will come unto thee quickly, and will fight against them with the sword of my mouth. Christ exhorts them to change their attitude ASAP, or else He will discipline them suddenly with His Word. God does not tolerate impurity in His church for long (Acts 5:1-11; 1 Cor. 11:27-32).

4. What He Promises (vs. 17)

*He that has an ear, let him hear what the Spirit says to the churches...*Our Lord extends two promises to *overcomers: hidden manna and a white stone!* The first speaks of the sufficiency of Christ, the second of our intimacy with Him. The victorious Christian is promised the glorious benefit of intimate communion with Christ – free from condemnation [A *white stone signified acquittal in ancient courts of law*] (Rom. 8:1)! What unspeakable joy – receiving a personally engraved gem-stone from Jesus Christ?! Even Rhudy's Jewelry can't beat that!

HISTORICAL NOTES ~ THYATIRA

(From Son of Man Vision, by Duane Spencer)

Of the seven cities...Thyatira was the smallest and least important. It was located in the mouth of a very strategic valley, through which major highways ran to Constantinople and Damascus, yet it did not enjoy the commerce of either Pergamos or Smyrna.

In fact, it began as a military outpost, which was designed to hold back the enemy until Pergamos could prepare her defenses.

There was one area, however, in which this city enjoyed commercial prominence – the wool and dye trade. Lydia, the "seller of purple" was from Thyatira (Acts 16:14). Her "purple" product was a very expensive dye, selling for about $300.00 per pound. It was almost worth its weight in gold!

Thyatira had its share of powerful trade guilds, which created many a crisis for early Christians, for the guild sponsored banquets served food previously offered to pagan idols (1 Cor. 8:10).

The name means, "unwearied sacrifice," and historically Thyatira pictures the Middle Ages and the ascendancy of the Roman Catholic Church, for in those days the organized church was indeed a Jezebel.

D. Christ speaks to the Church at Thyatira (2:18-29)

1. Who He Is (vs. 18) The *Son of God* here presents Himself as one with *Eyes like a flame of fire and feet like fine bronze.* He is the executor of searching judgment who will trample His enemies (vs. 27; 1:15). He is the omniscient and righteous evaluator of the church! The next few verses tell us His thoughts about Thyatira, but what would His searching eyes see in *your* church and *your* life, dear friend?

2. What He Knows (vs. 19-25)

a. Commendation (vs. 19) Few churches would want to be measured against Thyatira for her record of *works, love, service, faith and patience.* The phrase, *"and the last more than the first",* means that this church outdid herself in the arena of good works. However our Lord remains intolerant of evil...

b. Criticism (vs. 20-21) Thyatira is rebuked for allowing a false prophetess to openly advocate immorality and idolatry much like Jezebel of old, the gentile wife of King Ahab who promoted Baal worship (1 Kgs. 16; 2 Kgs. 9). Indulging such seductive heresy (1 Tim. 4:1) is born of hell itself and results in the sin unto death (1 Jn. 5:16; 1 Cor. 5:5) [physical death as divine discipline, <u>not</u> a loss of salvation].

3. What He Commands (vs. 22-25) *The deep things of Satan* (vs.24) refer to his counterfeit truths and pseudo-spirituality used to lure people from the riches of Christ (1 Cor. 2:10). Immediate repentance is urged! The Lord expects them to stop tolerating open sin and idolatry (Acts 15:28, 29) and to *hold fast until I come.* He is not done with His Church yet. He said, *"the gates of hell shall not prevail against it!"* Though everything around us is sinking into a moral cesspool, we must hold on! Jesus Christ is coming back soon!

4. What He Promises (vs. 26-29) Here the Overcomer is promised ***power over the nations;*** to rule and reign with Christ in the Millennium; to be co-shepherds (vs.27) in administering His will; and to receive the order of ***the morning star*** (cf. Rev. 22:16), a heavenly Medal of Honor! Halleluiah to the Lamb!

E. Christ Speaks to the Church at Sardis (3:1-6)

By way of quick review, let's suggest a one-word description of the seven churches in Revelation 2 & 3:

Ephesus	"Familiarity"
Smyrna	"Fear"
Pergamum	"Tolerance"
Thyatira	"Complicity"
Sardis	"Hypocrisy"
Philadelphia	"Discouragement"
Laodicea	"Self-sufficiency"

This church, as typical of so many churches in these last days, had a great <u>past,</u> but no <u>present,</u> and that is tragic! As Christ addresses the Sardis church, we see:

1. Who He Is (vs. 3a) *"These things says He Who has the seven Spirits of God and the seven stars."*

a. The reference to *"the seven Spirits of God"* has the Holy Spirit in view (compare 1:4). Since Christ is a co-equal Member of the Triune Godhead, He is the Possessor of the Spirit with His seven-fold character as described in Isaiah 11:2 (*"The spirit of the Lord...the spirit of wisdom and understanding, the Spirit of counsel and might, the spirit of knowledge and of the fear of the Lord.)*

b. Further, He has authority over *"the seven stars"*, the seven angels or messengers of the churches (see our note on page 26). In his commentary on Revelation Dr. John Walvoord states, "The same description of Christ as holding the seven stars in His right hand was given in relation to the letter to the church at Ephesus in 2:1 to make clear that the leaders of the church are responsible to no human representative of Christ and must give account directly to the Lord Himself."

The purpose of this description is intended to remind the members of this church that, though they may be fooling others with a supposed reputation of aliveness, they are not in any way fooling the Head of the Church! He employs the omniscient Holy Spirit and the ministering messengers to know all about His Church!

2. What He Knows (vs. 1b) *"I know your works, that you have a name that you live, and you are dead."* Indeed, what good is a reputation of life when there is only death? This condition is mindful of the condition of God's people in Isaiah 3:24, "Instead of sweet fragrance, there shall be rottenness".

Except for a few who had *"not defiled their garments"* (vs. 4), there was nothing commendable about this church – how tragic! They were reputed to be vibrant, having fabricated an attractive "visibility" through various external activities, but they were dead, and there's <u>nothing</u> more dead than **dead orthodoxy!** Oh, how the modern church needs to ponder this indictment!

3. What He Commands (vs. 2-4)

   a. *"Be watchful"* This is a command to be cautious, pay strict attention, and take heed. The Lord is telling them to recognize and admit their error!

   Paul makes a similar command to the Corinthian church in 1 Corinthians 16:13 – *"Watch, stand fast in the faith...be strong."* And Peter, warning against our adversary, the devil, tells us to "Be sober, be vigilant..."

   b. *"Strengthen the things which remain, that* are ready to die..." This is a wake-up call to re-emphasize the few evidences of life they still had. This is a significant warning in light of the city of Sardis itself! Once a strong city surrounded by deep cliffs virtually impossible to scale, Sardis was in a period of decline, as was the church there. What about <u>your</u> church? What about <u>your</u> life?

   c. *"Remember, therefore...and repent"* Much the same as our Lord's command to Ephesus in 2:5, this serious indictment demands a radical and decisive change! Verse 3 is saying, "Deal with your disobedience <u>now</u>...If you don't God will deal with it suddenly and unexpectedly!"

Verse 4 provides a reassuring statement from Jesus, *"You have a few names even in Sardis who have not defiled their garments, and they shall walk with Me in white, for they are worthy."* Praise the Lord for the faithful few! Their fidelity of character and faithful service will one day have its outward manifestation.

4. What he Promises (vs. 5-6) *"He that overcometh, the same shall be clothed in white raiment; and I will not blot his name out of the book of life, but I will confess his name before My Father, and before His angels. He that hath an ear, let him hear what the Spirit saith to the churches."*

An Important Reminder: [1] The unsaved *never* overcome; [2] The Christian *always* overcomes *positionally;* [3] The Christian *may or may not* overcome *experientially.*

As to the promise *"I will not blot his name out of the book of life"* this is not a threat of loss of salvation (if it was, salvation would be by works, not by grace!). There are two possibilities in this promise:

[1] Jesus makes an explicit statement that no believer will ever have his name blotted out of this book of life.

[2] Some say that the book of life is a list of all for whom Christ died, thus all who have possessed physical life. If they fail to trust Christ for salvation, their names will be removed from the book (compare Phil. 4:3; Rev. 13:8; 17:8; 20:12, 15; 21:27).

F. Christ Speaks to the Church at Philadelphia (3:7-13)

Today, this city in Turkey is called Alasehir. It was originally named for Attalus Philadelphia, the king who built it. The name comes from the Greek word *phile,* meaning "brotherly love" or "brotherly kindness". In its early days, the pagan god Dionysius was worshipped in Philadelphia.

1. Who He Is (vs.7) Stating that He is *"holy"* and *"true"*, having *"the key of David"*, Jesus is assuring the suffering saints at Philadelphia that He is aware of all unrighteousness and untruth and has Sovereign power to protect His own *("He opens and no man shuts; and shuts, and no man opens.")* This One Who has the "key of David" will in fact sit on the Throne of David in the Millennial Kingdom "to order it and to establish it with judgment and with justice from henceforth even forever." (Isaiah 9:6-7). Indeed, God the Son is in absolute control of all history!

2. What He Knows (vs. 8) *"I know thy works; Behold I have set before thee an open door, and no man can shut it; for you have a little strength, and have kept My word, and have not denied My name."* The indication is that these saints, though discouraged by the barrage of opposition, refused to deny Christ. They publicly proclaimed loyalty to Him and His Word without one moment thinking of "throwing in the towel".

Walvoord states, "The testimony of the Philadelphian church was divinely ordained by God and assured by His power and sovereignty. It is significant that the testimony of this church continued through the centuries in evident fulfillment of His promise that they should have an open door." Oh, that our churches today could have such a testimony!

3. What He Commands (vs. 9-11) Before issuing His command to *"hold that fast which you have"* (continue to maintain a firm grasp on your faithfulness to Christ, even under persecution), the Lord makes three specific promises, which will encourage believers to endure under trial:

[1] Christ promises the humiliation of the Church's enemies (vs.9). Unbelieving Jews of Philadelphia had attacked the church with violence, denouncing God's people to the civil authorities (compare Acts 17:5-9; 1 Thess. 2:14-16). God's Word promises that the day will come when deniers of the Faith will have to acknowledge the Truth (read Isa. 45:23; Rom. 14:11; Phil. 2:10-11).

[2] Christ promises to keep the Church *"from the hour of temptation"* (literally, "Trial" or "Testing", referring to Daniel's "70th Week", Dn. 9:24-27, the 7 year Tribulation following the Rapture of the Church) *which shall come upon all the world, to try them that dwell upon the earth."* Revelation chapters 6 through 18 give the details regarding this future event. Also read Joel 2:1-11; Zephaniah 1:14-18.

[3] Christ promises to *"come quickly"*. The thought is not that the Lord would come soon after His letter was written to Philadelphia, but that <u>when</u> He comes, He will come suddenly with great speed. As described in 1 Cor. 15:51-52, it will be "in a moment, in the twinkling of an eye." What a comfort to suffering Christians! What an encouragement to stand fast, knowing that Christ's coming is soon!

In light of these promises God's people are to *"hold fast"*, remain firm and true to Christ! As James said to suffering believers, *"Be ye also patient* (steadfast, enduring*), establish your hearts; for the coming of the Lord draweth nigh".*

4. What He Promises (vs. 12-13) In addition to the above promises Jesus declares, *"Him that overcometh will I make a pillar in the temple of My God, and he shall go no more out; and I will write upon him the name of My God, and the name of the city of My God, the new Jerusalem, which cometh down out of heaven from My God; and I will write upon him My new name."* What a glorious promise! Peter speaks of us as "living stones" (1 Pet. 2:5), but here the over-comer (all regenerated, blood-washed saints are overcomers positionally) will be <u>a pillar</u> in the heavenly temple, the New Jerusalem (Rev. 21:1-2). All who are identified with Jesus Christ will one day have this Blessed Savior identified with them! *"He that hath an ear, let him hear what the Spirit saith to the churches"* (God's personal challenge to you and me).

G. Christ Speaks to the Church at Laodicea (3:14-22)

Locate this city on your Bible map. A city of great wealth, it was located 40 miles from Philadelphia on the road to Colosse. Its main industry was the making of wool cloth. Its wealth and self-sufficiency had become the attitude of the <u>lukewarm</u> church there.

1. Who He Is (vs. 14) Reminding this miserable church of the finality and sovereignty of the One True God, Jesus call Himself—*"the Amen, the faithful and true witness, the beginning of the creation of God."* While this church is failing, Christ never fails (read Isa. 65:16; 2 Cor. 1:20; Rev. 1:5). While they are blind, He sees all (Heb. 4:13); while they are naked, He is clothed with majesty and honor and strength (Ps. 93:1; 104:1).

2. What He Knows (vs. 15) *"I know thy works, that thou art neither hot nor cold..."* Tragically, there is not one word of commendation for this assembly of Christians! What about <u>your</u> church? What about <u>your</u> life and witness? It is so important to realize that **Jesus knows!** This worldly church had become nauseous to God! They were smug and complacent. While they had not apostatized from the faith into an icy opposition, neither had it become inflamed with heated zeal. They were drifting, not driving! Again, what about you and me???

Note: The contrast here is between the hot medicinal waters of Hieropolis to the north and the cold refreshing waters of Colosse to the south.

3. What He Commands (vs. 16-19)

Threatening this church with complete rejection, Jesus says, *"I will spew thee out of My mouth"*. With their proud claims to self-sufficiency and their ignorance of spiritual bankruptcy (vs. 17), the Lord counsels them to *"buy of Me gold* (speaking of true faith, 1 Pet. 1:7) *...and white raiment* (speaking of righteousness to cover their spiritual nakedness) *...and anoint your eyes with eye salve* (restoring the visual vision they lacked). They are commanded to *"be zealous...and repent"*, accepting God's rebuke (vs. 19).

4. What He Promises (vs. 20-22) While verse 20 is often used in evangelistic invitations to the lost, Jesus is here speaking to His Church: *"Behold, I stand at the door and knock."* To the repentant one who opens the door of his heart, there is the promise of renewal of fellowship and power. For those who respond, this Blessed Savior, so neglected by so many, promises <u>present</u> blessings and an <u>eternal future</u> sharing His victory by sitting with Him on His throne! Glory, Hallelujah! By all means, *"He that has an ear, let him hear what the Spirit says"!!!*

WILL THE CHURCH GO THROUGH THE TRIBULATION?

"NO", For the Following Reasons:

1. The Tribulation is an Old Testament revelation regarding God's wrath against the Gentile Nations and His judgment of Israel (Ps. 50)

2. The term "God's wrath" is used to refer, not just to the final 3 ½ years, but also to the entire Tribulation period.
  a. Read Isa. 13:6-16 (esp. vs.9); Jer. 10:10; Zeph. 1:14-18; 1 Thess. 5:1-9; Rev. 6:16, 17.
    b. "Wrath" is used in at least 6 ways in Scriptures:
      (1) Man's wrath against man.
      (2) God's wrath against man (Jn. 3:36)
      (3) The Lake of Fire (Rom.5:9; 1Thess. 1:10).
      (4) The entire 7 year Tribulation as revealed in the above passages, especially 1 Thess. 5.
      (5) The first half of the Tribulation (Rev.6:16, 17).
      (6) The last half of the Tribulation (Rev. 11:18; 14:10, 19; 15:1 – here, God's wrath is said to be "filled up", not excluding any prior expressions of wrath).

3. The Church is not once mentioned in Rev. 6-18, the primary N.T. teaching on the Tribulation.

4. The word "caught up" in 1 Thess. 4:17 includes the reality of being rescued from sudden danger (probable reference to the Tribulation).

5. The term "Day of the Lord" in 1 Thess. 5:1-9 refers of necessity to ALL SEVEN YEARS, because no one will be saying "peace and safety" after the sixth seal is opened. The assurance of this passage is that the Church will have been "caught up" when the Tribulation begins.

6. There are NO SIGNS preceding the Rapture, thus precluding the Church going through any part of the Tribulation. Reminder: The signs of Matthew 24 all refer to what must occur prior to Christ's Second Advent to earth (during the Tribulation).

7. Christ's return for the Church was always considered imminent by the New Testament writers. There are no necessary events to precede Christ's catching out of His Bride, The Church. Read 1 Thess. 1:10; 4:17, noting that Paul includes himself by the word "we". He, as did John (1 John 2:28-3:3), fully expected Christ to return in his lifetime.

III. Vision of the Consummation, 4:1- 22:5
"The things which shall be hereafter..."

Chapter four begins the final section in our three-fold outline of Revelation (see 1:19). This portion is itself divided into three principal subjects: the Tribulation period (4:1-19:21); the millennium (20:1-15); and the eternal state (21:1-22:21). Chapters 4 & 5 serve as the prologue. From this point on, the events unfolding occur after the Rapture of the Church.

A. Prologue: A Throne, A Scroll, and A Lamb (4:1-5:14)
1. A Throne (4:1-11)

a. The Summons from the Throne (vs.1) *After this I looked, and, behold...in heaven...*

Literally, "after these things" refers to the letters to the seven churches in particular, and to the end of the Church Age in general. In chapters two and three, we saw the church on the earth. No more! The scene now shifts to heaven, where John is given a vision of God's glory before he witnesses the horrible judgment coming upon the world. What is recorded here is future, not only to John, but also to us. But not for long...Jesus is coming for His Bride very soon!

Behold is a watchword used often by John. It means, "to observe carefully for your own benefit," and reminds us of the promised blessing in 1:3!

(1) A Door was Opened. In 3:8, there was a door of opportunity for service for Christ. In 3:20, the door of our heart opens the way for intimacy with Christ. Here we see a doorway to heaven opened to provide John with insights necessary for him to understand God's prophetic plan. This heavenly door will open again for the Coming of Christ (19:11).

(2) A Voice was Speaking – *the first voice which I heard was as it were of a trumpet talking with me...* This is the same voice which spoke to John in 1:10. It is the clarion call of the Lord Jesus, calling His servant to *Come up here!* What a picture of our "blessed hope"! Remember, it is the trumpet call of the Lord which will call His Bride, the Church, to heaven (1 Thes. 4:16; 1 Cor. 15:51,52). Enoch was "caught up" to heaven before God's wrath was poured out on the earth. We believe the Church will likewise be delivered from the wrath to come (1Thes. 1:10; Rev. 3:10**). That's why the Church is not seen on the earth in the rest of the book!**

(3) A Promise was Given *...and I will shew thee things which must be hereafter*. I am reminded of Genesis 18:17, where, before God's wrath fell on Sodom, He called His friend Abraham aside and confided in him, *Shall I hide from [you] what I am about to do?* Before the Lord described his intentions to judge wicked Sodom, he first reiterated His promise. Now, God is revealing future judgment to John, but bolsters his faith with His promise and a vision of His Throne! Never forget, dear reader, Biblical prophecy is future history – recorded before it occurs – but just as certain as the ancient past. The events described in Revelation are not figments of John's imagination, but Jesus' unveiling what He is about to do!

b. The Sight of the Throne (vs. 2, 3)

(1) Its Setting – Heaven! *And...I was in the spirit [cf. 1:10]: and, behold, a throne was set in heaven...* Once again the Holy Spirit takes complete control of John. In this ecstatic, supernatural state, John is allowed into God's Throne-room. One commentator writes, "John was at once lifted above all that is natural and placed among divine things, his whole soul being filled, illuminated and occupied by these."

Revelation is a "throne book," [the word is used 40 times – *17 in chapters 4 and 5]* reflecting God's sovereign authority over the universe. Regardless of how circumstances appear in this world, God still rules. Psalm 47:8 says, *"God reigns over the heathen; God sits upon the throne of His holiness."* (cf. Esther; Ps. 103:19; Isa. 46:9-10).

*Was set...*speaks of that which is firmly fixed...secure and safe. This is in stark contrast with the kingdoms and thrones of earthly kings.

(2) Its Sovereign – Glorious! *And the One sitting [on the throne] was to look upon...*Who is this? Since the Spirit is "before the throne" (4:5), and the Lamb is "in the midst of the throne" (5:6), this must be God the Father (cf.5:7; 6:16; 7:10). Also compare Daniel's vision (Dan. 7:9). The sight of God's throne is always a blaze of indescribable glory:

like a jasper stone – This crystal clear jewel speaks of God's infinite purity (cf. 21:11; 23) In Ex. 28:20, it is the stone of Benjamin, the son of my right hand (cf. Heb. 10:12; Rev. 5:7).

like a Sardis stone – The blood red gem (named for the city) depicts God's redemptive grace (Rev. 21:20). In Ex. 28:17 it is the stone of Reuben, the first-born. Compare with "the first-begotten of the dead" (Heb. 1:6; Rev. 1:5). Spencer says, "In keeping with Hebrew thought, we may assume that this listing of the first and the last stones in the breastplate of the high priest infers the inclusion of all of the other tribes in between. We must conclude, therefore, that the

One who sits upon this throne is identified with the twelve tribes of Israel."

like a rainbow – The emerald rainbow appears (Ezek. 1:28), before the Tribulation (Rev. 6-18) begins, a reminder of God's faithfulness (Gen. 9:13-15). Mauro writes, "Sufficient for our purpose to state that the rainbow is, for those who see it, evidence that the storm has already passed over the spot whereon they stand." For those around the throne, there is no fear of the coming judgment – only awe at the glory and power of God!

c. The Scene around the Throne (vs. 4-11)

(1) The Twenty Four Elders – vs.4 *And round about...were twenty-four seats...and twenty-four elders sitting, clothed in white raiment; and they had on their heads crowns of gold.* Who are the elders? Ryrie explains it best, "Most pre-millennial scholars understand them to be individuals who represent all the redeemed. In the NT, elders as the highest officials in the church, do represent the whole church (Acts 15:6; 20:28), and in the OT, the same number of elders were appointed by King David to represent the entire priesthood (1 Chr. 24)...Others see [them] representing the church only. This appears to be more probable, since it is likely that Redeemed Israelites will not be resurrected until the second coming of Christ, at the end of the Tribulation (Dan. 12:2)."

In addition, the word for "crowns," *stephanos,* is used of Church Age believers' rewards in 1 Cor. 9:25; 1 Thes. 2:19; 2 Tim. 4:8; Jam. 1:12; and 1 Pet. 5:4. White raiment is attributed to glorified saints, not angels, in Revelation.

(2) The Seven Lamps of Fire – vs. 5 *Out of the throne proceeded lightnings and thunderings and voices: and* *there were seven lamps of fire burning...the seven Spirits of God.* Lightning etc., speak of judgment rumbling toward the earth! The text itself tells us that the burning lamps are a reference to the Holy Spirit of God in His seven-fold perfection (cf. Isa. 11:2; Rev. 1:4). Father, Son and Holy Spirit are involved in the impending judgments...just as all were involved in creation.

(3) The Crystal Sea of Glass – vs. 6a

In Ezekiel's vision of the throne (Ezek. 1), "crystal" describes the firmament, which is seen supporting the throne of God. Perhaps the glassy sea is not a sea at all, but the atmosphere which surrounds the earth and upon which the throne or judgment of God rests (cf. Isa. 66:1)

"Sea" speaks of judgment and is the heavenly antitype of the bronze laver in the tabernacle and the temple (Ex. 30:18; 2 Chr. 4:2, 6). That the sea is undisturbed in heaven, speaks of our fixed state of holiness in glory. There will be no more need of daily cleansing from sin (1 Jn. 3:2, 3). Halleluiah!

One thing is certain, glass as clear as crystal was as rare as gold in John's day. This scene must have filled him with absolute wonder.

(4) The Four Living Creatures – vs. 6-8a *Each [has] six wings and were full of eyes...*

These are not "beasts" as the KJV describes them, but magnificent, living angelic beings like the cherubim of Ezek. 1:5-14; 10:20 and the seraphim of Isaiah 6:2-3. Their description represents the four-fold character of Christ as seen in the Gospels:

*...like a lion – **Christ the King (Matthew)**
*...like a calf –**Christ the Servant (Mark)**
*...like a man –**Christ's Humanity (Luke)**
*...like an eagle – **Christ's Deity (John)**

(5) The Worship of God – vs. 8b-11

The ceaseless exaltation of the holiness of the Triune Godhead by the cherubim (vs. 8) has become the basis for many hymns and songs and is the first of fourteen doxologies in Revelation!

"Worship" is an expression of profound reverence in which we prostrate ourselves before Almighty God. It literally means to "ascribe worth."

Thus, the second doxology, ***Thou art worthy, O Lord, to receive glory and honor, and power.***

These magnificent beings exist for one purpose – to praise and glorify the Lord (vs. 11). In fact, that's why we ***all were created!*** Are you living for His pleasure or yours, beloved?

2. A Seven-Sealed Scroll (5:1-4)

It is important to understand the 4th and 5th chapters of Revelation as containing *the key* to the rest of the book. These chapters announce the Sovereign Triune God Who, prior to the glorious earthly reign of Christ; will execute judgment on all unbelievers. This judgment, the 7-year Tribulation, is revealed in graphic detail in chapters 6 through 18. Take a moment to read Zephaniah 1:14-18 and Matthew 24:21-22 (Our Lord's description of this period).

a. John's Vision (vs. 1) *"And I saw in the right hand of Him that sat on the throne a book written within and on the back, sealed with seven seals."*

The One on the throne is God the Father (chp. 4), and He is holding a seven-sealed book (literally, a "scroll" or "document", usually of parchment, animal skin, or papyrus). This scroll is later to be opened by *"a Lamb"* (vs. 6), Jesus Christ Himself. The scroll was so full and detailed that it required both front and back. Chapter 6 will reveal that the destiny of this sin-cursed world is divinely signed and sealed!

b. The Angel's Question (vs. 2-3) "And I saw a strong angel proclaiming with a loud voice, Who is worthy to open the scroll and to loose its seals?" A comment by J.B. Smith in his book, *A Revelation of Jesus Christ,* is that "The angel proclaims with a loud voice (denoting) urgency and great concern...Who is the strong angel making the challenge? The answer is doubtless Gabriel, the one who ordered the closing and sealing of the book to Daniel."

While verse 3 declares sadly that *"no man in heaven, nor on earth, neither under the earth, was able to open the scroll, neither to look on it,"* verses 5 and following will reveal and exalt the One Who is both *"worthy"* and *"able"*. This is *"The Lord Who is worthy to be praised"* (Ps. 18:3), the One Who is *"worthy of more glory than Moses"* (Heb. 3:3). Is He able? Does His ability impact our lives today? Oh, YES! Read on...

"God is able to make all grace abound toward you, that you always, having all sufficiency in all things, may abound to every good work." (2 Cor. 9:8)

"Now unto Him Who is able to do exceedingly abundantly above all that we ask or think, according to the power that works within us" (Eph. 3:20).

"Now unto Him Who is able to keep you from falling, and to present you faultless before the presence of His glory with exceeding joy" (Jude 24)

Also, take a moment to read 2 Tim. 1:12 and Heb. 2:18. Indeed, no man is worthy nor able, except THE MAN, CHRIST JESUS! Praise God for the great God-Man!

62

c. John's Reaction (vs. 4) *"And I wept much, because no man was found worthy to open and to read the scroll..."* John's uncontrollable sobbing and sorrowing points out man's inability to do what only God can do. It appeared to John that no one was capable of revealing what was in the scroll.

3. A Lamb (5:5-14)

In these verses the One Who alone is worthy to open the 7-sealed book is both clearly identified and gloriously worshipped.

a. The Lamb Identified (vs. 5-7) *"and one of the elders (see note at 4:4) said to me, Weep not; behold, the Lion of the tribe of Judah, the Root of David, has prevailed to open the scrolls, and to loose it's seven seals".* John is told to stop crying and to fix his eyes on the One Who is worthy and able.

(1) He is identified as Israel's Messiah, *"the Lion of the tribe of Judah"* (compare Gen. 49:8-10), and *"the Root of David"* (read Matt. 1:1; 21:42-43). These descriptions emphasize Christ's strong and noble Kingship over His Jewish people in fulfillment of the Davidic Covenant (2 Sam. 7:10-16).

(2) He is identified as the Church's Savior (vs. 6-7), called *"A Lamb as though it had been slain..."* His redemptive work at Calvary is completed; He now stands in all His majesty, having conquered death!

"...having seven horns (symbolic of omnipotence, full strength; see ps. 18:2; 75:4-10; Zech. 1:18) *and seven eyes, which are the seven Spirits of God..."* (symbolic of complete omniscience, all-knowingness; see Zech. 3:9; 4:10). *"And He came and took the scroll out of the right hand of Him Who sat on the throne."* In receiving the scroll from the Father, the

fact of judgment and power being committed to Christ is now confirmed (John 5:22 states that *"The Father has committed all judgment to the Son"*. Compare Daniel 7:13-14, where Christ's ultimate triumph is declared).

b. The Lamb Worshipped (vss. 8-14) Three different groups fall down before Him:

(1) Worship of the Cherubim and the Twenty Four Elders (8-10). Here is revealed angelic beings and regenerated human beings as they jointly *"fell down before the lamb, having every one of them harps* (or lyres, only one of two instruments, along with the trumpet, spoken of in heavenly worship) *and golden bowls full of incense, which are the prayers of saints"*. How important to Almighty God are the prayers of His children! He looks on them as sweet-smelling incense, a symbol of acceptance and pleasure in Scripture (compare David's prayer in Psalm 141:2).

In **verses 9 & 10** *"they sang a new song"*, which magnified the Lamb's worthiness to open the sealed scroll. <u>Four reasons</u> are given for the worth of the lamb: **(a)** He died. **(b)** He purchased our redemption with His blood. **(c)** He gave the redeemed, including us, a position before God as *"a kingdom of priests"* compare 2 Pet. 2:9; Rev. 1:6); **(d)** He will allow us to *"reign on earth"* with Him in the millennial kingdom.

(2) Worship of the Angelic Hosts (11-12) While the Bible makes no reference to angels singing, they are heard here making a joyful noise, as a numberless multitude shout with a loud voice this seven-

fold ascription of worshipful praise: *"Worthy is the Lamb that was slain too receive power, and riches, and wisdom, and strength, and honor, and glory, and blessing."* Can we do less??

(3) Worship of Every Creature in Heaven and On Earth (13-14)

Compare Phil. 2:8-11, where we see the father exalting the Son and <u>every </u>knee, including the unsaved, bowing to Him. The Cherubim and the 24 elders join in this "Hallelujah Chorus". Truly, Christ is worthy!!!

B. Vision of the Seven Seal Judgments (6:1-8:1)
And I saw when the Lamb opened one of the seals, and I heard...the noise of thunder, one of the four [living creatures] saying, Come and see.

<u>Note the change in "scenery"</u>
> Chapters 1-3 take place on earth;
> Chapters 4-5 take place in heaven;
> Chapter 6ff shifts back to earth.

John's vision now looks forward to Christ's future judgment that will take place after the close of the Church Age. This begins the great day of God's wrath. As the seals are opened, the most terrible time in history unfolds. It will be a brief but intense seven years, the 70th week of Daniel 9:27. As the Lamb breaks each seal, a rebellious humanity faces the weight of God's Justice against sin.

The Tribulation period contains three series of judgments, which follow one another in order: the seals (6), the trumpets (8,9) and the bowls (16). The intervening chapters reveal key facts about the period that are not arranged chronologically. Chapter 7 encompasses the entire period. Chapter 18 spotlights one event (Babylon's destruction), while 11 (the two witnesses) surveys the first half of the period.

Ryrie summarizes, "The chapters in this section are not unlike a phone conversation. They start telling the story in order (6), but soon there is an interruption to fill in some information (7). Then the order of events is resumed (8,9) only to return to some more fill-in (10-15). There is a return to the progressive order of events (16) and finally more detail (17-19). Sometimes the "fill-in" material runs ahead of the story; at other times it backs up to add or emphasize pertinent information."

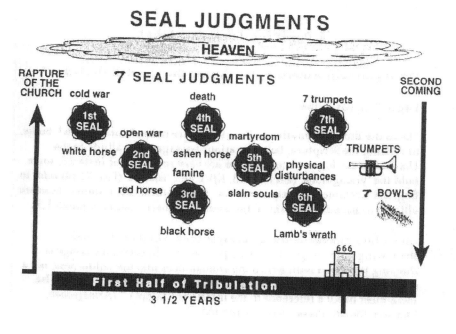

1. The 1st Seal: *A White Horse* (6:1, 2)

...Behold a white horse: and he that sat on him had a bow; and a crown was given to him: and he went forth conquering, and to conquer.

A white horse speaks of peace and majesty. This is, however, not the same as Christ the Conqueror, seen on His white horse at Armageddon in Rev. 19:11ff. The crown worn by this rider (stephanos – "wreath crown") is different from that in 19:12 (diadema polla – "many crowns"). Here, the rider holds a bow, whereas in 19:15 Christ wields a sword!

But, "a bow and a crown" does fit the biblical descriptions of the Antichrist – a military leader and benevolent dictator who rises to power as a peacemaker (2 Thes. 2; Dan. 9:29). His conquering appears to be an initial international acceptance of his authority over a 10-kingdom federation of western nations (the ten-toed image of Dan. 2:40-43 and the "ten horns" of Dan. 7:7, 8, 15-23; Rev. 13: 1 and 17:3).

This "cold war" conquest (*without arrows)* corresponds perfectly with the delusion of peace and safety which describes the beginning of the Tribulation in 1 Thes. 5:3. He rules for 42 months after his true identity is revealed (13:5).

2. The 2ⁿᵈ Seal: *A Red Horse (6:3, 4)*

"And there went out another horse...red: and power was given to him...to take peace from the earth...that they should kill one another: and there was given unto him a great sword."

Depicting bloodshed and open war, the second seal reveals another aspect of the first half of the Tribulation – *Satan is not omnipotent! He cannot deliver on his false promises of world peace!* Murder by violence, revolutions and chaos will abound in his kingdom. All the king's horses and all the king's men (even the United Nations) won't be able to forge a lasting peace. If they could, we wouldn't need Jesus!

In 2 Thes. 2:7-8, only the gracious intervention of the "Hinderer" (the Holy Spirit working through the Church) maintains any semblance of a peaceful world today! He is restraining sin while patiently waiting for souls to turn to Christ

(2 Pet. 3:9). But when the Church is Raptured and the restraining ministry of the Holy Spirit is removed -*Watch Out!*

3. The 3rd Seal: *A Black Horse* (6:5, 6)

"And lo, a black horse; and he that sat on him had a pair of balances in his hand...a measure of wheat for a penny, and three measures of barley for a penny; and see thou hurt not the oil and the wine."

The black horse depicts worldwide famine. The "balances" reveal that, in spite of efforts to ration food supplies, wholesale starvation will occur.

The Roman denarius, or coin, was equal to a day's wages for a laborer in Palestine in Jesus' day (Mt. 20:2). Ordinarily it could purchase ten quarts of wheat or thirty of barley. In this time of famine, there will be one-tenth the normal supply of food! So, a daily wage will buy food for only one person, and families will suffer terribly.

Luxuries ("oil and wine") will be hard to get or impossible to buy, increasing man's frustration.

4. The 4th Seal: *A Pale Horse* (6:7, 8)

"And behold a pale horse: and his name that sat on him was Death, and Hell followed with him. And power was given unto them over the fourth part of the earth, to kill with sword, and with hunger, and with death, and with the beasts of the earth."

Following war and famine, we see one fourth of the population of the earth destroyed! Think of it! By today's census that would mean 1.5 billion people will die – just from the judgment of this one seal!!!! That is beyond our capacity to fathom. The world has never seen such a catastrophe – not even when the "black death" plagued Europe. And this doesn't even include the millions or billions that will die from the chaos and starvation of Seals 2 and 3. And the worst is yet to come (cf. 9:15).

This ashen horse (a sickening pale green, almost yellowish) points to death itself. The Greek word for "pale" is *kloros*, from which we derive our modern word "chlorophyll" (green, cf. Rev. 9:4).

The "sword" in 6:8 *(hromphaia – a Thracian sword)* is different from that of the second horseman *(machaira – the Roman two-edged, short sword)* in 6:4. Regardless, it seems evident that the bloodshed of the second seal continues and brings even more death to the earth.

Thus the Four Horsemen of the Apocalypse ride onto the stage of history, leaving a swath of destruction and havoc in their wake. Satan's great attempt to rule the world in Christ's stead is doomed to failure! Man's pride will bring him to the doorway of Hell.

5. The 5th Seal: *Slain Saints of the Tribulation (6:9-11)*

"And when he had opened the fifth seal, I saw under the altar the souls of them that were slain for the Word of God, and for the testimony which they held."

In the opening of this seal the scene changes from earth to heaven, as John is given a vision of those who will be cruelly killed during the first half of the Tribulation. The reason for their martyrdom is their bold and unwavering testimony for Christ. Such spiritual fervor is desperately needed today!

The question is often asked, "Will anyone be saved during the seven year Tribulation?" Verses 10 and 11 provide a strong "YES", as do such passages as 7:9-10, 13-14; 12:17; and 14:1-5. Even as God is pouring out His wrath on unbelieving and Christ-rejecting people, millions will come to saving faith in Christ!

In response to the martyrs' question, *"How long, O Lord...do you not avenge our blood...?"* God will dress them in *"white robes"* and tell them, in effect, to leave all vengeance to God and to *"rest yet a little season",* because many more of their brethren were yet to die for the faith. Their white robes signify, not only their redemption, but that they have a temporary body suited for their presence in heaven (read 2 Cor. 5:1). This body will be replaced by their everlasting resurrection body at Christ's return. Dr. John Walvoord in his commentary states:

"There have been many martyrs in every generation, and even in the twentieth century tens of thousands have died for Christ in Asia, Africa, Central America, and South America. There are several reasons, however, for believing that a greater period of martyrdom is yet ahead."

6. The 6th Seal: *Universal Political and Ecological Upheaval (6:12-17)*

"And I beheld, when he had opened the sixth seal and, lo, there was a great earthquake, and the sun became black as sackcloth of hair, and the moon became like blood, and the stars of heaven fell unto the earth."

Here indeed, and in the verses that follow, are all the elements of God's wrath poured out in catastrophic judgment! These, as some want to say, ARE NOT mere symbols of havoc. Take a moment to read such parallel passages as Joel 2:10-11, 31; Amos 5:18-20; and Zephaniah 1:14-18.

Verses 14-17 add another note to this judgment of God. He will open heaven itself (vs. 14), apparently to allow the unsaved to get a fear-striking glimpse of the God of their judgment. They will unsuccessfully attempt to commit suicide as they try to hide *"from the face of him Who sits on the throne, and from the wrath of the Lamb; For the great day of His wrath has come, and who shall be able to stand?"*

This reference to "the great day of His wrath" reveals the ushering in of the second half of the Tribulation (see Christ's words in Matthew 24:21-22).

****

Note: **The 7ᵗʰ seal is opened in 8:1, revealing the seven Trumpet judgments. Chapter seven is considered a parenthetic interlude in events.**

A QUESTION EVERYONE ASKS!

What part will America play during the Great Tribulation?

Edgar C. James writes:

"Does the Bible say anything about the future of the United States? Some, in reading the Scripture, believe various passages may allude to the United States. But such conclusions are very remote. For instance, some hold the "young lions (Ezek. 38:13, KJV), and "islands" (Psa. 72:10) refer to England's colonies; namely, America. But a careful check shows those are villages or islands of Tarshish, the area of southern Spain (cf. Jonah 1:3).

Others find America as the "great eagle" (Rev. 12:14) or the "land shadowing with wings" (Isa. 18:1 KJV). But the Revelation passage is showing the speed with which the woman flees into the wilderness, not a nation. The Isaiah passage refers to a nation with "whirling wings" (Isa. 18:1), most likely a reference to the insects of Ethiopia. (Armageddon, Chicago: Moody Press, 1981, pp. 102-103).

However, simply because the United States is not mentioned in prophecy does not mean it has no role in the latter days. To the contrary, it would appear tragically possible the United States will function as the most important member of the Antichrist's ten-nation Western confederation.

THE MARTYRDOM OF POLYCARP

The courageous testimony of Polycarp is especially noteworthy at this juncture in our study of Revelation, as we consider the harsh reality of the cost of following Jesus during the Tribulation period (6:10-11; 7:9-17; 11:9-10; 12:11; 13:7, 15-17).

Smyrna, representing the era of the persecuted church (A.D. 100-313), has a legacy of martyrdom that must not be forgotten. The city had a large, Jewish population. The leaders of the Synagogue of Smyrna were intent on ridding their city of all the followers of the Prophet, whom they had rejected as their Messiah. These events set the stage for the martyrdom of Polycarp, beloved bishop of the Church of Smyrna, and a disciple of the apostle John.

On a local feast day, Polycarp was ordered to worship Caesar, or die. Polycarp gave his immortal reply, *"For 86 years I have served Christ, and He has never wronged me. How can I blaspheme my King who saved me?"*

A scream of rage went up from the mob, which demanded his death. He shouted, *"I do not fear the fire that burns for a season and is finally quenched! Why do you wait? Come, do your will!"*

As the flames embraced him, he was heard to pray, *"Lord, I thank Thee that Thou hast graciously thought me to be worthy of this day and hour, that I may receive a portion in the number of martyrs, in the Cup of Thy Christ."*

IMPORTANT NOTE:

The chronological narrative of chapters six and eight is now interrupted by the scene revealed in Chapter seven. From the severity of God's wrath that is demonstrated in the first six seals, it is natural to wonder if anyone at all will be saved during the tribulation period (6:17). But we must remember that God's grace always precedes God's judgment – and that His justice is always tempered with mercy.

Chapter seven, a "parenthetical interlude" in the progressive outpouring of God's judgment, answers this question with hope and promise! Not only will 144,000 Jews be saved and sealed, but their ministry on the earth will apparently result in the salvation of a world-wide multitude of Gentiles. Halleluiah! What a Savior! Even in the hey-day of Satan's deceptions, under the rule of the Anti-Christ, the Gospel of Jesus Christ will still be *the power of God to salvation to everyone who believes, to the Jew first and also to the Gentile* (Romans 1:16). Never forget, dear saints, that the Word of God declares, *Greater is He that is in us, than he that is in the world* (I John 4:4).

FIRST PARENTHETIC SECTION

THE REDEEMED OF THE TRIBULATION (7:1-7)

1. THE SEALED JEWS (7:1-8)

2. THE SAVED GENTILES (7:9-17)

THE CHRONOLOGY
OF
<u>REVELATION</u>

The Tribulation period contains three series of judgments which follow one another in order: *The Seals (6), The Trumpets (8-9), and The Bowls (16).*

The intervening chapters reveal key facts not arranged chronologically:

-Chapter 7 encompasses the entire seven years.

-Chapter 11 surveys the first half of the period.

-Chapter 18 spotlights Babylon's destruction.

Ryrie describes the chapters in this section as a phone conversation: they start telling the story in order **(6);** an interruption fills in some information **(7);** the order of events resumes **(8-9);** followed by more fill-in **(10-15);** the progressive order of events resumes **(16);** and finally more detail **(17-19).**

Sometimes the "fill-in" material runs ahead of the story; at other times it backs up to add or emphasize pertinent information.

NOTE THESE PARALLELS

Matthew 24	*Revelation 6*
False Christs (4-5) --------White horse/false peace (1-2)	
Wars (6) --------------------------------Red horse/war (3-4)	
Famines (7a) --------------------Black horse/famine (5-6)	
Death (7b-8) ---------------------- Pale horse/death (7-8)	
Martyrs (9) --------------- Martyrs under the altar (9-11)	
World chaos (10-13) ---------------World chaos (12-17)	

Matthew 24:14 introduces the preaching of the Gospel of the kingdom throughout the whole world, and this may well be where Revelation 7 fits in. God may use the sealed 144,000 Jews to share His Word with the world, resulting in the salvation of multitudes.

1. THE SEALED JEWS (7:1-8)
a. The Suspension of Judgment (vs. 1-3)
(1) Instruments of Suspension (vs. 1-2)
And after these things I saw four angels standing...
(a)Angels of the Four Corners These angels are not identified by name, but are God's holy angels charged with controlling nature (14:18; 16:5).

They stand in contrast with the four "bound" *fallen* angels (demons) seen in 9:14. I like to refer to them as *the Southwest-*

76

ern Angels, because of the SW region known as "Four Corners" where four states join (Arizona, Colorado, New Mexico, and Utah)!

The *four corners of the earth* represent the four cardinal directions of the compass and the divinely established trade winds of the earth (which blow with such regularity of motion and direction that sea-going vessels use them to navigate).

(b) Angel from the Rising Sun – *And I saw another angel ascending from the east* (literally, "from the rising of the sun"), *having the seal of the living God…*Again, this angel is not named, but his authority (Eph. 3:10; 6:12) suggests Gabriel the "announcing angel" (Dan. 8:16; 9:22; Luke 1:19) or Michael (Dan. 10:13,21; 12:1; Jude 9; Rev. 12-7). This angel of the East has a special mission. He is God's envoy sent to set apart His servants for their tribulation ministry.

(2) Instructions re: Suspension (vs. 2-3)

(a) Delay Judgment – *and he cried with a loud voice to the four angels…saying, Hurt not the earth…till we have sealed the servants of our God in their foreheads.* All judgment is suspended until this protective seal (refer to pg. 70 for the significance of this seal) marks God's envoys. God's grace always precedes His judgment.

(b) Don't Harm Land, Sea, Trees

(3) Intent of the Suspension (vs.3)

(a) Seal God's Servants (Ezek. 9:14)

(b) Significance of Sealing (Rev. 13:16)

These sealed ones are owned by God and they are kept by God. God will ensure their physical safety from all harm until their mission is completed. What is their mission?

Why this special sealing? Refer to the notes on pages 66, 69 for further insights.

b. The Sum of the Jews (7: 4-8)

(1) 12,000 Jews from 12 Jewish Tribes –

Taking language in its ordinary sense, we must understand these 144,000 to be literal people from the 12 tribes of Israel – clearly Jewish tribulation saints.

(2) Three Problems with the Listed Tribes
- **Why is the tribe of Levi included?**
- **Why is Ephraim not included?**
- **Why is Dan omitted?** We don't know for sure, but it may be because of the sins of idolatry practiced by Dan and Ephraim (1 Kg. 12:25-28).

TWO GROUPS OF PEOPLE
IN
REVELATION CHAPTER SEVEN

7:1-8   7:9-17

Jews – *one* nation ------Gentiles – from *all* nations

Numbered – 144,000-------- Impossible to number!

Sealed on earth --------------- Standing in heaven –
    By Angels   before God

While we are not told explicitly in Scripture that the 144,000 Jews are God's special witnesses, and that the Gentile host is saved through their ministry, this appears to be a logical deduction; otherwise, why are they associated in this chapter? The parallel with Matthew 24:14 also indicate that the 144,000 will witness for the Lord during the Tribulation.
(Wiersbe's *The Bible Exposition Commentary, Vol.II, pg. 590)*

WHAT IS GOD'S SEAL?

"Saying, Hurt not the earth, neither the sea, nor the trees, until we have sealed the servants of our God in their fore-heads." – Rev. 7:3

The Greek word **sphragis** has the idea of the branding of cattle and the tattooing of slaves and soldiers. Those in the service of the emperor could be recognized by this mark if they deserted.

Soldiers and guild members were marked on the hand, brow, or neck to be sealed as a sign of consecration to the deity [or emperor].

The significance of sealing *(visible or invisible)* was to mark ownership and security **(cf. Eph. 1:13; 4:30).**

Ryrie's notes on Ezekiel 9:4, state that "a mark" is literally a taw, the last letter of the Hebrew alphabet – written at the time *like a cross!* Persons so marked would be spared in the destruction of Jerusalem. Similarly, God will mark the 144,000.

Remember that Moses commanded the people of Israel to "mark" their doorposts with blood in Exodus. This mark *(forming the outline of a cross)* protected the Jews from the angel of death.

Also, the "mark of the beast" (Rev. 13:15-18) is Satan's counterfeit of God's seal. It too signifies ownership and protection. However, the mark of the beast will be unable to deliver the wicked from the wrath of the Lamb (Rev. 6:17).

2. The Saved Gentiles (7:9-17) In this first parenthetic section, John is given to see the sealed Jews of the tribulation in 7:1-8 and the saved Gentiles in 7:9-17. For those who question whether people will be saved during the Tribulation, here is the once-for-all answer!

a. The <u>People</u> Who Are saved (vs.9)
(1) Their number *"...a great multitude, which no man could number"* (beyond all human computation!)

(2) Their identity *"of all nations* (a reference to Gentiles) *and kindreds* (literally, "tribes:, a clear reference to Israel, this, Jews) *and peoples* (of various nationalitites) *and tongues* (different language groups)"

(3) Their activity *"stood before the throne* (where God the father sits) *and before the Lamb* (the resurrected Lamb of God, Christ Himself), *clothed in white robes* (revealing their redemption), *and palms in their hands* (emphasizing their rejoicing). Compare 6:9-11, probably a parallel reference to martyred saints of the Tribulation period, as they are revealed to be in 7:13-14.

b. The _Praise_ of Those Who Are Saved (vss. 10-12) Indeed, what a glorious "hallelujah Chorus" we see here as redeemed saints and holy angels lift their voices together in a great symphony of praise!
(1) Their crescendo of praise (10) *"Salvation to our God Who sits upon the throne, and unto the lamb."*

(2) Their companions in praise (11 – 12) In these verses all the angelic host and the 24 elders (see their identity in our notes on 4:4) and the four living creatures (the cherubim) fall jointly before God, worshipping Him along with the multitude of martyred saints (vs.9). Read the 7-fold ascription of praise to God in verse 12 and join your voice to these! Compare the praise of Rev. 5:12).

c. The _Period_ in Which They Are Saved (vss. 13-14) This great multitude of verse 9 come out of that future period called *"The great Tribulation"*. While many will die during the 1st half (6:7-11), the "Great Tribulation" has specific reference to the final 3 ½ years of the 7 year "Day of the Lord" (Joel 1:15; 3:14; Zephaniah 1:7, 14; Matthew 24:21). Review the chart below:

d. The _Provisions_ of Those Who Are Saved (vss. 15-17)

(1) Their service is unending! (15) _"...serve Him day and night"_

(2) Their satisfaction is unbounded! (16) _"hunger no more...thirst no more"_, plus no harmful exposure.

(3) Their sufficiency is unlimited! (17) _"The Lamb...shall feed them, and shall lead them unto living fountains of waters; and God shall wipe away all tears..."_

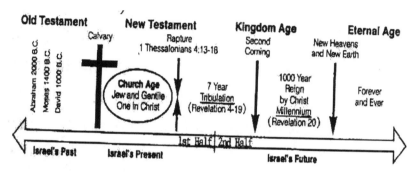

7. The 7th Seal: 7 Trumpet Judgments (8:1)

And when he had opened the seventh seal, there was silence in heaven about the space of half an hour. With the opening of the seventh seal, the trumpet judgments are announced after a period of solemn silence – a pregnant pause accenting the impending doom. These trumpets, heralding a successive crescendo of God's wrath unleashed upon the world, are so terrifying that the heavenly hosts are stunned into silence.

> **NOTE:** The first six judgments are announced in Chapters 8 and 9. The seventh judgment (11:15-19) follows another parenthetical section (10:1-11:14). In addition, the first four trumpet judgments primarily affect nature (earth, sea, rivers, and sun), while the last three are poured out on unrepentant man (9:21).

C. Vision of the Seven Trumpet Judgments (8:2-11:19)

Refer back to 6:17, where, following the release of the Seal Judgments, the second half of the Tribulation is announced. The Trumpets, and all that follows, occur during the last half of Daniel's Seventieth Week (a seven year period), called by Christ *The great tribulation* in Matthew 24:41 (the first three and a half years are referred to as, *The beginning of sorrows* in Mt. 24:8).

1. The First Trumpet: *Earth is Burned* (8:2-7)
a. Angelic Preparation (vss.2-6) *And I saw the seven angels which stood before God; and to them were given seven trumpets.* These *angels* are not named but they appear again in 15:1 and 21:9.

Trumpets are frequently mentioned in relation to important events in the life of Israel (Ex. 19:6; Num. 10: 1-10, Jer. 4:5). Throughout history trumpets have always heralded the approach of royalty – that's why a great trumpet will announce the coming of Christ for His Church (1Cor. 15:51-52; 1 Thes. 4:16)! Even in our culture, the entrance of the head of state is accompanied by "Hail to the Chief".

There is no reason to see *another angel* as other than a literal angel assisting in the prayers of God's people (described as *incense before God* in vss. 3 and 4) and in administering judgment (v. 5; cf. 2 Thes. 2:6-9). Angels are involved with answered prayers (Dan 10: 10-13, 20-21; Acts 12:7); but this <u>does not</u> mean we are to pray to angels (Col. 2:18)!

Voices, thunderclaps, lightnings, and an earthquake (v.5b) are a prelude to impending judgment, like dark thunderclouds before a storm. They are God's warning to man to repent – *while there is time* (read: Acts 17:30, 31; 2 Pt. 3:3-10)! <u>Principle:</u> God's grace always preceeds His judgment.

b. Divine Devastation (vs. 7) *The first angel sounded …hail and fire mingled with blood…the third part of trees was burnt…and all green grass burnt.* The plagues in Egypt were literal (Ex. 7-10) – so will these judgments be. In Genesis 1:11-12, plant life was the first to be created after the heavens and the earth.

Now, the first trumpet will burn 1/3 of all vegetation! The earth will become a scorched, desert wasteland!

2. The Second Trumpet: *Oceans become Blood (8:8-9)*
…a great [burning] mountain was cast into the sea…the third part…became blood; and a third of the creatures…died; and a third of the ships were destroyed. Can you imagine? This appears to be a burning, mammoth meteor or a huge volcanic eruption (such explosions have been known to render local water supplies bitter and unfit for consumption). Compare Exodus 7:19-21! Apparently, whatever strikes the sea creates a tremendous *tsunami*, which sinks 1.3 of the world's oceangoing vessels, undoubtedly causing economic and military havoc.

3. The Third Trumpet: *Fresh Waters made Bitter (8:10-11)*

*...and there fell a great [burning] star...called Worm-wood...and a third of the waters became [bitter] and many men died...*God created and named all the stars (Job 9:9). This judgment comes from a flaming meteor, which will poison 1/3 of the world's fresh water supply, including underground springs. *Wormwood* is a bitter Mid-east shrub and a symbol of bitter sorrow (Prov. 5:4).

4. The Fourth Trumpet: *Day/Night Cycle Broken (8:12-13)*

...the sun...the moon...and the stars; so that a third [were] darkened...and I beheld an angel...crying...Woe, woe, woe!

On the fourth day of creation light appeared; with the fourth trumpet, the light of the world dims (Ex. 10:21-23)! *Was smitten* means to strike a calamitous blow. Calamity indeed. But the worst is just around the corner!

THE FIRST TRUMPET

HAIL, FIRE, BLOOD
⅓ Earth on Fire
⅓ Trees Burned
All Grass Burned

THE SECOND TRUMPET

FALLING METEOR
Destroys
⅓ Ships
⅓ Fish
⅓ Sea filled with Blood

THE THIRD TRUMPET

FALLING STAR
Poisons
⅓ of all
Water on Earth

THE FOURTH TRUMPET

SUN, MOON & STARS
⅓ of Sun, Moon
& Stars DARKENED

THE FIFTH TRUMPET

LOCUSTS
5 Months of
Torture by
Scorpion Stings

THE SIXTH TRUMPET

SATAN'S ARMY
200 Million
Warriors
Kill ⅓ of
Mankind

THE SEVENTH TRUMPET

EARTHQUAKE
7000 Die in
Jerusalem
People Run
to Mountains

5. The Fifth Trumpet: *The Demonic Locusts (9:1-12)*

As cataclysmic as the first 4 trumpet judgments will be, the final 3 will be far worse! Read 8:13, in which John sees an angel proclaiming with a loud voice, *"Woe, woe, woe, to the inhabiters of the earth by reason of the other voices of the trumpet of the three angels which are yet to sound!"* Thus, the final three trumpet judgments are called "woes".

>   *a.*   **The Depression from which They Come (vss. 1-2)** *"The bottomless pit"*
>   **(1) The creature who releases them** *"And the fifth angel sounded, and I saw a star fall from heaven unto the earth…"*

The verb "fall" is in the perfect tense and should read "having fallen". The "star" is identified in verse 11 as **Satan** and he is seen here as having already fallen. Isaiah 14:12-15 records his moral ejection from heaven when he, as Lucifer, attempted to exalt his authority over God. While he is still able to appear before God as "the accuser of the brethren" (Rev. 12:10), he will be once-and-for-all ejected by Michael the archangel during the Tribulation period (Rev. 12:7-9).

>   **(2) The crater from which they are released** *"and to him was given the key of the bottomless pit. And he opened the bottomless pit, and there arose a smoke out of the pit…and the sun and the air were darkened…"*

This deep depression, probably adjacent to hell in the bowels of the earth, is always seen as a holding place for demonic beings whose ultimate fate will be in the lake of fire (Rev. 20:10, 14-15). This bottomless abyss is referred to in 9:1, 2, 11; 11:7; 17:8, 20:1, 3. It is also mentioned in Luke 8:31 and Romans 10:7. It is here that Satan will be confined during the thousand year reign of Christ on earth (20:1-3).

b. The Destruction which They Cause (vss. 3-6)
"...power as the scorpions of the earth..."

(1) Their power is strictly limited (3-4a) As is revealed in verses 3-6, the character of this 5ᵗʰ trumpet judgment is that of demonic depression. While, under God's sovereign control, these locust-like demonic creatures are given to exercise power, they are not allowed to ***"hurt the grass of the earth, neither any green thing, neither any tree..."***.

Commenting on the identity of these "locusts", Ryrie states, "They are animal creatures, like locusts, though not ordinary locusts, for they are demonic in nature. Indeed, it would be better to describe them as demons who take the form of these unique locusts. Verse 11 makes it clear that this is the cast." A.S. Peake, in his commentary, adds" "These descriptions of heaven and hell were meant by the author to be taken very literally...The scorpion locusts are quite literally intended; they are not heretics, or...Mohammedans, or...the Jesuits, or Protestants...but they are uncanny denizens of the abyss, locusts of a hellish species, animated by devilish instincts and equipped with infernal powers."

To appreciate the way God uses locusts in the Bible to execute judgment, take a moment to read Exodus 10:12-15 and Joel 1:4-7; 2:1-11.

(2)Their power is strategically focused. (4b-6) While their power is limited as to all green vegetation and trees, they are commanded to ***"hurt...those men who have not the seal of God in their foreheads."***

Tormenting unsaved people in a way comparable to the dreadful sting of a scorpion, their power is focused in that those sealed by God are excluded. Dr. John Walvoord states that this protection "may extend as far as this plague is concerned to <u>all</u> who know the Lord in that day." Praise the Lord for 2 Timothy 2:19 – "The foundation of God standeth sure, having this seal, the Lord knoweth them that are His."

Walvoord continues, "In a similar way, believers in the present age are sealed with the Holy Spirit of promise according to Ephesians 1:13-14. It would seem improbable that any true believer in that day would be subject to the torment of the locusts; the torment is rather a judgment upon Christ-rejecting men."

Verse 5 states that these demonic locusts will torment the unsaved for *"five months"* (compare vs. 10). In those days it is said that the ordinary time during which locusts destroyed crops was 5 months. There is no reason to see this torment in any other way than a literal 5 months (imagine a scorpion sting lasting 5 months!).

So agonizingly horrible is this judgment of God that verse 6 says, *"In those days shall men seek death and shall not find it; and shall desire to die, and death shall flee from them."* Undergoing such incessant pain will surely cause these people to seek death by suicide! However, as is common in demonic affliction, those in the grip of demons are not free to exercise their ability of free choice. Even the hope of death to escape their agony is removed from them in this dark hour to come!

c. The Description by which They are Identified (vss. 7-12)

(1) They have symbolic likeness. (7-10) It is strategic here to notice the repeated use of the word *"like"* in these verses (7 times). These various likenesses are intended to manifest their fearful and destructive appearance. *"The shapes* *of the locusts were like horses...on their heads crowns like gold...faces like the faces of men..."* (etc. etc.)

Indeed, it may be difficult to even imagine such creatures, this is a literal description of these powerful and ferocious demons. No wonder this is called the first woe!

(2)They have Satanic leadership (11-12)
"And they had a king over them, who is the angel of the bottomless pit, whose name in the Hebrew tongue is Abaddon, but in the Greek tongue hath his name Apollyon."

Both of the above names are translated "Destroyer". Isn't it revealing of the mighty power of God, that He will include the use of Satan to bring judgment on those who refuse and reject the Savior, Jesus Christ!

Though in our day Satan appears often as an angel of light (2 Cor. 11:14), here the mask is stripped away. He is a Destroyer!

6. The Sixth Trumpet: Four Demons and Their Vast Army (9:13-21)
   a. The Release of Demons (vss.13-   14)
     (1)The four-horned golden altar
The altar of mercy ~ the altar of judgment.
     (2)The four demons of the great river.
     Those bound are now loosed.

The Euphrates River

- **The longest and most important river in the Middle East**
- **One of four rivers of the Garden of Eden (Gen. 2:14)**
- **Nearby, the first lie was told, the first murder committed, and the tower of Babel built**

- **The eastern boundary of the Promised Land (Gen. 15:18; Ex. 23:31; Deut. 11:24)**
- **Israel's influence extended to the Euphrates under David/Solomon (1 Chr. 18:3;2 Chr. 9:26)**
- **This region was the central location of three world powers that oppressed Israel: Assyria, Babylon, Medo-Persia.**
- **On it's banks Israel endured 70 years of captivity (Ps. 137:1-4)**
- **The enemies of God will cross this river enroute to the Battle of Armageddon (16:12-16)**

b. The Return of Death (vss. 15-19)

Under the judgment of the first "woe," or fifth trumpet, men were not allowed to die, but now death returns with a vengeance in the second "woe"!

(1) God's Timing (vs. 15) *And the four angels were loosed, which were prepared for an hour, and a day, and a month, and a year...*

These unidentified four arch-demons may be those to whom Satan delegated responsibility for influencing the four major world empires of Babylon, Medo-Persia, Greece and Rome (Dan.2 & 7; 10:20). These flag-rank demons will be released by the sovereign will of God as part of His divine judgment – at the precise moment He has chosen – not a minute before (cf. Dan. 9:24-27)! Don't forget beloved, Satan could not even touch Job without God's permission.

The result? *... for to slay the third part of men.* The destructive power of the evil emissaries is described here and in verse 18. The present population of the world is approximately 6 billion souls. Under the judgment of the "pale horse" (6:8), one-fourth of all humanity will die (1.5 billion), leaving 4.5

billion behind. That means that another 1.5 billion will perish as these demonic executioners are unleashed. Thus, the combined total of the fourth seal and the fifth trumpet judgment equals fully one-half (3 billion) of our current population! If that doesn't arrest your attention, think of it this way: *3 billion was the total population of the earth in 1970!*

(2) Satan's Teeming Horde (vs. 16-19)
Now, from the seat of Satan's greatest victory (the Garden of Eden), comes the greatest army and the greatest slaughter the world has ever seen.

(a) Their Tally – *And the number of the armies of the horsemen...two hundred thousand thousand...*
John MacArthur states that the plural form of **armies** implies that this host will be divided into four armies, each commanded by one of the previously bound demons (*Revelation* 1-11, pg. 271). The total force is an astounding 200 million strong! As far back as the 60's, major periodicals reported Red China's boast that they had a combined military force of **200,000,000!** It is feasible that an oriental coalition could field such a massive army today. No one in the first century could have imagined such a host on the field of battle. But, two thousand years ago, God knew and revealed it to John. If the Joint Chiefs of Staff want to plan for future operations, they need to check out the Bible!

Some believe this to be the great army of the East mentioned in Revelation 16:12. Regardless, this army is energized by demonic power!

(b) Their Terror...*and I heard the number of them. And I saw...breastplates of fire, and of jacinth, and brimstone...and the heads of the horses were as the heads of*

lions; and out of their mouths issued fire and smoke and brimstone.

John's description of these horsemen is absolutely terrifying. The colors are the very colors used in the Bible to paint a picture of hell (Gen. 19:24-28; Rev. 14:10; 19:20; 20:10; 21:8). The color of *fire is red; hyacinth is dark blue/black like smoke; brimstone is a sulphurous burning yellow.*

Strauss's notes are worth quoting in their entirety here, "The weapons of this mighty power are fire, smoke, and brimstone. While they are the weapons of hell, they are nevertheless the emblems of God's judgment. Brimstone is a gas with a sulphurous smell. It was this stifling and strangling gas that God sent down from Heaven upon the city of Sodom when He destroyed it (Luke 17:29). The coming judgment upon Babylon will take on a similar form (Rev. 14:10), as will the judgment against the beast and the false prophet (Rev. 19:20), Satan (Rev. 21:8). What a ghastly place this earth will become when hell is let loose! It is but a sample of the torment that unbelievers must endure in hell forever. And to think that in those days there will be no one to help. If this message has reached anyone who is not yet saved, I urge you: receive Jesus Christ at once as your Lord and Savior" (*The Book of Revelation, pages 195, 196*).

(c) Their Toll – *And by these three was the third part of men killed, by the fire, and the smoke, and by the brimstone, which issued out of their mouths.*

The word *three* in the KJV is literally, *plaques* in the Greek text (cf. 11:6, 15:1,6,8; 16:9,21; 18:4,8; 21:9; 22:18) and refers back to the fire, smoke, and brimstone of the previous verse. This might also be a symbolic reference to modern warfare. Only time will reveal the exact details of this horrible, catastrophic judgment. But the carnage will make the world a graveyard.

The phrase a ***third part*** is used thirteen times in connection with the trumpet judgments – in connection with the earth and trees, the fish and the sea, the ships and the rivers, the sun, moon and the stars, and now mankind.

God promised He would never again judge the earth by a flood, but He also promised judgment by fire (Ps. 97:3; Isa. 66:15; Zeph. 1:18, Lk. 12:49, etc.).

(d) Their Tails – *For their power is in their mouth, and in their tails…like unto serpents…and with them they do hurt*

These images describe the supernatural deadliness of these demons in commonly understood terms. The sting of the scorpion results in convulsions and paralysis (9:5). Here the oppression of these spirit legions will madden men and drive them to battle and death.

c. <u>The Reaction of Defiance (vss.20-21)</u>

In the aftermath of such horrific events we would expect that all who survive would beg for God's mercy. Instead, the exact opposite occurs. Men will cling to their violence, sensuality, sorcery and idolatry. Evil will have become good, and good evil!

(1) Refusal to Turn from Pride and Idolatry (vs.20)

(2) Refusal to Turn from Violence and Immorality (vs.21)

The Hardness of Man's Heart

But the rest of [unsaved] mankind, who were not killed by these plagues, did not repent of the works of their hands, that they should not worship demons, and idols of gold, silver, brass, stone, and wood, which can neither see nor hear nor walk. And they did not repent of their murders or their sorceries or their sexual immorality or their thefts. **Rev. 9:20, 21**

This stubborn arrogance demonstrated by all of unsaved humanity (under the influence of the Anti-Christ) when facing the direct, supernatural judgment of Almighty God against wickedness in the Great Tribulation is reminiscent of the intransigence of homosexual predators (Gen. 19:4, 11-12) and of Pharaoh's unrepentant attitude toward God's plagues on Egypt (Ex. 5:2; 7:3-4; 11,13-13, 22-23; 8:15,19,32; 9:7,12,34-35; 10:1,20,27; 11:10; 14:5f, 17-18).

Repentance is the Greek word, *metanoieo*, which means "to change one's mind or thinking; to turn about/reverse directions." Sinful man will knowingly reject the truth of Jesus Christ because of their insatiable desire for money *(thefts),* violence *(murder),* pornography (*Porneia* = general term for *sexual immorality*/perversion), and the occult (Grk. Pharmakia = *drugs & witchcraft).* Read carefully Romans 1:18, 21, 24, 25, 28, 32; 2:5. Wicked men who no longer fear the judgment of God (Rom.3:18) will stand condemned by Nineveh (Mt. 12:41-45). Only those who turn from the worship of Satan (Rev.13:4, 8) and trust solely in the Lord Jesus Christ will have hope (Acts 26:14-18; 1Ths.1:9,10; Rev.20:13-15).

Vs. 20 – [They] repented not of:
- *The Works of their Hands (Gen. 4:3-7)*
- *The Worship of Demons (Deut.32:17; Ex.20:3; Mt.4:8-10)*
- *The Worship of Idols (Gen.11:26 w/ Joshua 24:2; Gen.31:19,34; Ex.20:4)*

Vs. 21 – Neither repented they of:
- *Murder (Gen.4:8-11; 6:11, 13; Ex.20:13)*
- *Sorcery (Deut.18:9-13)*
- *Sexual Immorality (Gen.9:22; 19:5,35; Ex.20:7)*
- *Stealing (Gen. 27:13:23; 37:23; Ex. 20:8, 17)*

(cf. Gal.5:19f; Rev.18:23; 21:8; 22:15)

The sins listed in Revelation 9:20, 21 include violations of the 1st, 2nd, 6th, 7th, and 8th commandments of God (Ex.20). Violation of even one makes man guilty of all before a Holy God (Jam.2:10).

These five sins represent the whole of man's defiance of truth and the total lawlessness which will characterize a world gone mad after the one who bears the title, "The Man of Lawlessness" in 2 Thes.2:3.

These evil practices will undoubtedly be the libertarian creed of the apostate world church (Rev.13:11ff) of the Tribulation period. That such vile things could be justified in the name of religion is made apparent by the endorsement of "homosexual marriages" by main-line faith-groups today (cf. Ps.2)!

7. The Seventh Trumpet: *The Triumph of Christ (11:15-19)*

a. The Pronouncement of the Angel (vs.15)

The Pronouncement of the Angel in Rev.11:15

(Fulfillment of many Old Testament Prophecies)

"The kings of the earth set themselves, and the rulers take counsel together, against the Lord, and against His Anointed, saying, Let us break their bands asunder, and cast their cords from us. He Who sits in the heavens shall laugh; the Lord shall have them in derision." **(Psalm 2:2-4)**

"...and the government shall be upon His shoulder...Of the increase of His government and peace there shall be no end, upon the throne of David, and upon His kingdom, to order it, and to establish it with justice and with righteousness from henceforth even forever." **(Isaiah 9:6-7)**

"And in the days of these kings shall the God of heaven set up a kingdom; which shall never be destroyed." **(Daniel2:44)**

"And the Lord shall be King over all the earth; in that day shall there be one Lord..." **(Zech.14:9)**

b. The Praise of the Twenty Four Elders (vss.16-18)
   (1) Praise for God's Reign (16-17)
   (2) Praise for God's Wrath (18)

c. The Presence of God (vs.19)
   (1) A Reminder of God's love, grace and mercy (19a)

(2) A Reminder of God's holiness, justice, and judgment (19b)

Regarding the Reference to "The Ark" in Revelation 11:19

In his commentary on Revelation, William R. Newell makes an interesting statement:

"I have sometimes been asked 'What became of the ark of the covenant when the temple was destroyed by Nebuchadnezzar? It surely must be preserved somewhere.' Human thoughts are surely not God's thoughts, for He distinctly tells us (Jeremiah 3:16) that in the future kingdom the ark shall not be remembered nor come into mind. Of course, the Apocrypha must have Jeremiah running and hiding the ark! (II Maccabees 2:1,8). Why is it that the very folks who thus inquire beyond what is written, concerning the temple of old, are filled with doubt concerning what is plainly written of the temple in heaven?"

SECOND PARENTHETIC SECTION
(10:1 - 11:14)

1. **THE ANGEL AND THE LITTLE SCROLL (10:1-11)**
2. **THE MEASURING OF THE TEMPLE (11:1-2)**
3. **THE ACTIVITIES OF THE TWO WITNESSES (11:3-14)**

It is important to note that, John having now received the vision of the SEAL judgments in chapter 6 and the TRUMPET judgments in chapters 8 & 9, we now come to the longest interlude (chapters 10-15) before the BOWL judgments of chapter 16. In these parenthetic chapters (10-15) a number of graphic events will be revealed to John, some of which will occur during the first half of the Tribulation and some during the second half.

1. The Angel and the Little Scroll (10:1-11)

In this parenthetic section John is given to see *"another mighty angel"*. After a description is given, this angel makes a powerful declaration, followed by some strange demands.

a. Description of the Angel (vss.1-2)

(1) His heavenly appearance (1) *"And I saw another mighty angel come down from heaven, clothed with a cloud; and a rainbow was upon his head, and his face was as it were the sun, and his feet like pillars of fire."*

This spectacular heavenly authority with such majestic brilliance has been given various identities by evangelical scholars. Some believe the description is much like that of Christ in Rev.1:13-15; others believe this mighty one to actually be a human messenger, though unidentified; however, most hold him to be an actual angel, and the description points to an angel, perhaps the same as spoken of in 5:2 (also, compare Dan.10:5-6). Dr. Harold Willmington prefers the identity to be Michael the Archangel, comparing him to Dan.12:1; Rev.5:2; 7:2; and 8:3. This angel's authority is obviously delegated by Christ Himself.

(2) His earthly authority (vs.2) *"And he had in his hand a little scroll open; and he set his right foot upon the sea, and his left foot on the earth."* Ryrie states, "This seems to present an image of conquest and to relate the angel and his ministry to God's purpose of taking possession of the entire world (land and sea), which will be worked out in the Tribulation period."

The little scroll referred to here is not clearly identified, but the contents seem to represent the written authority given by Christ to the angel to fulfill his mission.

b. Declaration of the Angel (vss.3-7)

(1) The seven thunders (vs.3-4) The angel's cry is so loud and authoritative that it is likened to the roar of a lion. Two events happen: **(a)** *"Seven thunders uttered their voices"*, pointing to the perfection of God's intervention in judgment. Compare Psalm 29:3-9, where the 7-fold voice of Jehovah is heard. **(b)** John *"heard a voice from heaven saying…Seal up those things which the seven thunders uttered, and write them not."* Thus, these voices from heaven seem never to have been recorded, being heard and seen only by John. The principle here, as confirmed in Deuteronomy 29:29, is that there are secrets which God chooses to withhold from man at certain times (compare Dan.8:26).

(2) The sovereign termination (vs.5-7). The angel whom John saw standing upon the earth and the sea now confirms with an oath the purpose of Almighty God, *"Who created heaven and the things that are in it…"* to lay claim to His rightful ownership and inheritance. The eternal, all powerful Creator will complete what He began!

The statement that *"there should be time (delay) no longer"* means that, in the final half of the Great Tribulation to come, there will be no more interval of time before the final outpouring of God's judgment issuing in Christ's return. When the seventh angel (11:15) sounds his trumpet, the horrible bowl judgments of chapter 16 will be immediately poured out. *"The mystery of God"* in verse 7 is the sacred truth concerning God which will not be revealed until His judgments are complete and His earthly kingdom established.

c. Demands of the Angel (vss.8-11)

(1) John is to take and eat *(8-10)* John is told to *"take the little scroll…"* and to *"eat it up; and it shall make thy belly bitter* (speaking of God's revelation of impending judgment) *but it shall be in thy mouth sweet as honey"* (speaking of God's revelation of love, grace, and mercy).

This activity of eating the scroll has an important application: Before God's prophet can minister His grace and judgment to others, he must let the Word of God impact his own life. By partaking of the contents of the scroll (God's Word), the prophet is appropriating the statements contained in the scroll, both the sweet mercy and grace of God and the bitter judgment of God to be poured out on the Tribulation earth. The obvious application for you and me is to allow God's precious Word to so affect our lives, as David expresses in **Psalm 19:9-10)**

"The fear of the Lord is clean, enduring forever; the judgments of the Lord are true and righteous altogether. More to be desired are they than gold, yea, than much fine gold; sweeter also than honey and the honeycomb."

Another passage that is similar is **Jeremiah 15:16** *"Thy words were found and I did eat them, and Thy word was unto me the joy and rejoicing of my heart."*

(2) John is to prophesy again (11)

"And he said to me, Thou must prophesy again about many peoples, and nations, and tongues, and kings."

Full and affected by the bitterness and sweetness of the scroll, John is commissioned to prophecy about a multitude of people and language groups. When is this to take place? The entire context reveals the time frame to be the final half of the Tribulation, called by Jesus *"The Great Tribulation"* (Matt.24:21-22). This powerful revelation of God will include both commoners and kings!

Jesus' words confirm the seriousness of this prophesy: *"Except those days should be shortened, there should no flesh be saved."* (Mt.24:22)

The first half of chapter eleven is a continuation and conclusion of the second parenthetic interlude (10:1-11:14) in the chronology of Revelation. Before introducing the two witnesses *[about whose identity there is more speculation than about any other fact of prophecy – with the possible exception of futile attempts to name the antichrist!]*, John is given instructions regarding the Temple.

2. The Measuring of the Temple (11:1-2) – *And there was given to me a reed like unto a rod: and the angel stood, saying, Rise, and measure the temple of God, and the altar, and them that worship therein.*

a. The Command (v.1a) – *Measure the Tribulation Temple.*

Here John is not only a witness of these Tribulation events, but a participant. He is given a **reed** *(Greek: kalamos)* or "measuring rod," which refers to a Jordan Valley cane-plant that grows to a height of 15-20 feet. It is light, hollow and rigid and was used for manufacturing items as diverse as pens (3 Jn.13 and walking sticks (Ezek.29:6), as well as for determining distance (cf.Ezek.40:5) where the reed was a yardstick of "6 cubits: or 9 feet).

No explanation is given of this command, but to **measure** something signifies ownership – even as we survey land today to determine boundary lines. John Walvoord believes the symbolism indicates that Israel is measured and falls short: "measuring the temple will indicate the apostasy of the nation…and their need for restoration." When the Great Tribulation begins the temple will be desecrated, sacrifices stopped and the worship of the antichrist will be enforced (Dan 9:27; Mt. 24:15; 2 Thes.2:4; Rev.13:14-15).

b. The Count (v.1b) – *Number the Worshippers*

The worshippers mentioned in John's vision represent the believing remnant of faithful Jews still living in Israel. God always has a remnant of faithful followers in every generation (1Kgs.19:18)! These may include the 144,000, as well as other tribulation Jews who will come to faith in Messiah before the end.

c. The Court (v.2a) – *Exclude the Outer Court given to the Gentiles*

This is a significant omission and refers to the court of the Gentiles, located just outside the area containing the brazen altar. Gentiles were forbidden to pass beyond this outer courtyard to enter the temple proper. In fact, Rome delegated to the Jews the right to execute any Gentile who trespassed and thus defiled the temple (Acts21:28-29). MacArthur writes,

"God redeems Gentiles, and will continue to do so during the tribulation (5:9; 7:9). But He will reject those believing Gentiles who have united with Satan…and oppressed His covenant people, Israel. The sharp distinction in this vision between Jews and Gentiles suggests that the church, having earlier been raptured (3:10), is not present during the Tribulation, because in the church, *there is no distinction between Greek and Jew, circumcised and uncircumcised* (Col.3:11; Eph.2:14-16).

d. The Contempt (v.2b) - *...it has been given to the nations; and they will tread underfoot the holy city* (Jerusalem) *for forty-two months* (3 1/2 years). The wolf's mask will come off at this time.

Ryrie points out, "Thus the functioning worship of the temple described in vs. 1,2 occurs during the first part of the Tribulation, whereas the treading down of the city by Gentiles [is] during the last 42 months." This will be when the "man of sin" breaks his peace treaty with Israel and terminates Jewish temple sacrifices by demanding that the world worship his image (Dan.9:27; Luk.21:24; 2Ths.2:4).

The Tribulation Temple

(Dr. Lehman Strauss' *Commentary*, pg. 211)

The language of chapter 11 is peculiarly Jewish and looks forward to the rebuilt temple in Jerusalem during the Tribulation. None of these details have been fulfilled. There is nothing in history to which we can point; it is all prophetic. That there will be a temple built in Jerusalem for the worship of Jehovah is proved by several passages. There were at least three temples built [in the past]: **Solomon's** (1Kgs.8), destroyed by Nebuchadnezzar in 583 B.C. (2Kgs.24-25); **Zerubbabels's** (Ezr.3), destroyed by Antiochus Epiphanies in 168 B.C.; and **Herod's**, referred to by our Lord in John 2:20, destroyed by Titus in 70 A.D.

This temple [Rev.11:1-2] is to be built in *the "holy city" [Jerusalem]...no other city is so designated in the Bible* (Neh.11:1, 18; Isa.52:1; Dan.9:24; Mt.4:5; 27:52-53). God is not finished with the Jews. A magnificent temple will be erected at Jerusalem...the priesthood and sacrifices will be [reestablished]. In that temple the personal Antichrist will appear and claim the right to be worshipped (2Thes.2:4). This is the abomination of desolation" (Dan.9:2; Mt.24:15). The world will accept him who will come in his own name (Jn.5:43; Rev.13:12-15).

3. The Activities of the Two Witnesses (11:3-14)

a. The Ministry of the Two Witnesses (v.3-6)

(1) The duration of their ministry (v.3) *And I will give power unto my two witnesses, and they shall prophesy a thousand two hundred and threescore days, clothed in sackcloth.* This 3 ½ year period (42 months, 1,260 days) is probably the <u>first half</u> of the Tribulation period since the Antichrist will kill them (v.7) at midpoint. Again God demonstrates His hand of mercy by sending two supernaturally empowered prophets to call on mankind to repent. Notice – their power *(authority)* comes from God, not man. [You know, when preachers lay hold of this simple truth it transforms their preaching and the people are blessed! But when men preach to please men, because they have forgotten their responsibility to God, the sheep starve and are scattered by the wolves.]

Sackcloth was a rough, burlap type cloth worn in the ancient world as a symbol of sorrow and mourning (Gen.37:34; 2 Sam.3:31; 2 Kg.19:1; Job 16:15; Dan.9:3). These two express God's great sorrow over the wickedness of the world gone mad after Satan. They mourn because of the defilement of Jerusalem, even as Christ lamented His beloved city (Mt.23:37).

(2) The dedication of their ministry (v.4) *These are the two olive trees, and the two candlesticks standing before the God of the earth.* A comparison of this verse with Zech.4:3, 11-14 reveals that the "olive tree" identifies these two as *God's anointed ones*, specially chosen for this critical time. "Candlesticks" refers to the character of the witnesses as *light bearers* during this dark hour.

Exactly who these prophets are is not specified...though one would never know that from all the sanctified speculations often heard! What is important to know about these men is what is revealed about their purpose (to bear witness of Almighty God, v.7) their power (miraculous signs, v.6) and their impact (the whole world will fear God, v.11).

(3) The devastation caused by their ministry *(v.5,6)* *And if any man [try to] hurt them, fire...devours their enemies...These have the power...that it rain not...to turn [waters] to blood, and to smite the earth with all plagues, as often as they will.*

Here is why many Bible teachers believe these two to be Moses and Elijah, for the miracles they perform follow the pattern of those performed by God through Moses and Elijah (Ex.7-12; 2Kgs.1:10,12; 1Kgs.17:1; Jam.5:17) who also appeared with Christ on the Mount of Transfiguration (Mt.17:3).

b. The Martyrdom of the Two Witnesses (v.7-10)

(1) The corruption causing their deaths (v.7-9) And when they shall have finished their testimony, the beast...shall kill them. And their dead bodies shall lie in the street of the great city...and shall not...be put in graves.

Only after God's purpose for them is complete can they be harmed (cf. Jn. 10:18; 19:30). Beloved, that is true for every believer – our life is not done until His purpose for us is finished, and nothing can touch us apart from His divine permission (cf. Job1:12; 2:6; Phil.1:6)!

The two witnesses [Grk. *Martus*] will literally be martyred in Jerusalem, the place where Jesus was crucified. Referred to earlier as "the holy city" (v.2), it is now compared with Sodom and Egypt because of the "abomination of desolation" in the temple. Now there is nothing holy left in Jerusalem and judgment comes (v.13; cf. Gen.18:20ff).

Apparently the news networks will be closely following these prophets and their disruption of the antichrist's global "harmony"! Around the world people will be glued to their TV sets vicariously participating in and cheering as they are executed "live." With modern satellite transmission the possibility of this has become a reality in our generation. Isn't it amazing that John saw this possibility 2,000 years ago?! [This is nothing less than a technological extension of the ancient Roman coliseums where men and beasts were routinely killed to slake the blood-thirsty of a decadent people.] In fact, after they die, there will be a morbid gloat-fest over their dead bodies (v.10).

(2)The celebration following their deaths (v.10) *And they that dwell upon the earth shall rejoice over them, and make merry, and shall send gifts to one another; because these two prophets tormented them…*

The death of the two witnesses will touch off a worldwide celebration that will be the antichrist's counterfeit Christmas. This response demonstrates the final hardening of men's hearts. Truly evil will have become good when the man of lawlessness rules the earth. Armageddon is just around the corner.

c. The Metamorphosis of the Two Witnesses (v.11-14)

(1) Resurrection: raptured to heaven (v.11,12) *And after three ½ days the Spirit of life from God entered into them, and they stood upon their feet; and great fear fell upon* *them which saw them. And...a great voice from heaven...Come up hither. And they ascended up to heaven in a cloud; and their enemies beheld them.*

While it is possible to silence Christ's witnesses, it is impossible to destroy the Truth which they proclaim. God's Word always accomplishes its purpose (Isa.55:11).

God cuts short this grotesque celebration by calling His servants' home in plain view of the whole world! By allowing the unsaved to witness this display of His power and victory over death, he provides a final warning to all who still dare to reject His grace.

The result of this miraculous resurrection will be a world-wide panic. Pure terror will grip men's hearts. There will be no doubt now in anyone's mind just Who has done this (Jesus Christ) and just what they are guilty of doing, and who it is who has deceived them (the antichrist).

(2) Destruction: earthquake in Jerusalem (v.13,14) A destructive earthquake devastates the city and brings glory to God.

110

> ### *Third Parenthetic Section (12:1-14:20)*
>
> The parenthesis beginning at 10:1 is interrupted by the 7th Trumpet, which is then interrupted by another parenthesis (the 3rd). This section deals with various "Tribulation Realities." It does not follow precise chronological order, but rather reveals important personalities and events that have a significant impact during the Tribulation period.

(1) Tribulation Realities: The Woman with Child (12:1-2)

And there appeared a great wonder in heaven; a woman clothed with the sun and the moon under her feet, and upon her head a crown of twelve stars: And she being with child cried, travailing in birth, and pained to be delivered.

A great wonder is literally "a great sign," an object with special meaning (cf.12:3; 13-13, 14; 15:1; 16:14; 19:20). A "sign" *(semeion),* is a person or event that looks beyond itself to some greater significance (e.g. *in John's Gospel, each sign points to the Deity of Christ).*

The Seven-Fold Use

of "Signs" in Revelation

1. (12:1) The sign of "a woman clothed with the sun…" = ISRAEL
2. (12:3) The sign of "a great red dragon" = SATAN.

3. 4. & 7. (13:13,14; 19:20) The *counterfeit* signs of the second "beast" who causes mankind to worship the antichrist = THE FALSE PROPHET.

5. (15:1) The sign of the "seven angels having the seven last plagues: = THE BOWL JUDGMENTS.

6. (16:14) The deceptive signs of the spirits of demons drawing the nations into the Battle of Armageddon = THE SIXTH BOWL JUDGMENT.

Here the Holy Spirit is clearly indicating that what is actually seen is symbolic of something else, and by comparing verses 5-6 with Gen.37:9-10 and Rom.9:4-5, it is clear that this *woman* is a reference to Israel, the birthplace of Messiah, *the man child*. In that OT passage we see the symbolic description of *Jacob as the sun, Rachel as the moon, and their sons* (the heads of the 12 tribes of Israel) *as their stars*.

What is in view here in 12:1ff is the dragon's (Satan's) persecution of the woman (Israel) during the last 3½ years of the Tribulation. This description of Israel reveals the great and final holocaust *(travailing…and pained to be delivered)* that is to befall the chosen people before the establishment of the Messianic Kingdom. Read Isaiah 66:7-10; Micah 4:10; 5:2-3; Romans11:11-15, 25-27.

NOTE: Beginning here, and continuing through chapter 13, seven personalities are seen crossing the prophetic stage of Revelation:

1. A Woman (Israel) 12:1-5

2. The Dragon (Satan) 12:7-17

3. The Man-Child (Jesus Christ) 12:4-16

4. The Arch-Angel (Michael) 12:7-9

5. The Remnant (Believing Israel) 12:17; 14:1-5

6. The Beast out of the Sea (Anti-Christ) 13:1-8

7. The Beast of the Earth (False Prophet) 13:11-17

(2) Tribulation Realities: The Great Red Dragon (12:3-4)

*And there appeared another sign in heaven; and behold a great red dragon…*The identity of the dreadful, fearful beast is clarified in verse 9, *the great dragon was cast out, that old serpent, called the Devil, and Satan, who deceives the whole world.*

The dragon's power and cruelty are indicated by the adjective *great.* His murderous and bloodthirsty nature is revealed in the descriptive color *red.*

The *seven heads* (global empire*)…ten horns* (10 kings heading a ten-nation coalition – like EU – under the antichrist's leadership)…*and seven crowns* (indicated the complete authority of antichrist's tyranny and the principal powers within the global empire – Rev.17:10) relate Satan to the Beast of 13:1

and reveals the superior knowledge, power, and authority he will wield. Daniel2:40-43, 7:7-8, 24, and Rev.17:12 make it clear that this dragon is the corrupt revived Roman Empire of the end times.

The phrase, ***his tail drew the third part of the stars of heaven…***in verse four is probably a reference to Satan's revolt against Almighty God when 1/3 of all the angelic hosts (Job38:7; Rev.9:1) joined him in his coup attempt (Isa.14:12-15; Ezek.28:12-19; 2 Pet.2:4; Jude 6).

…to devour her child reflects the historical record of Satan's efforts through Herod to kill the Christ-child (Mat.2:16-18; Rom.9:4-5).

The Fall of Satan

Originally named Lucifer (*Light Bearer, Brilliant One*, cf. Ezekiel.28:11-19), the Bible tells us that Satan was:

- The crown of wisdom and beauty (v.12-13)
- The praetorian of God's throne (v.14)
- Created without sin (v.15)
- Ruined by pride (v.16-17)

Lucifer's glory was merely the reflected glory of God. At some point, pride filled his heart and caused his downfall. Apparently, one third of all the angels were caught up in his seraphic sedition (Rev.12:4).

In Isaiah14:12-15, we find the five "I Will's" of Lucifer, which outline his revolutionary motives:

1. I will ascend into Heaven.
2. I will exalt my throne above the stars.
3. I will sit upon the Mount of Congregation in the sides of the North.
4. I will ascend above the Heights of the Clouds.
5. I will be like the Most High.

116

(3)   Tribulation Realities: The Male Child (12:5-6)

Here is revealed Israel's role in bringing the Messiah, who is destined to ***rule all nations with a rod of iron,*** into the world (Ps.2; Rev.2:27; 19:15).

When we read...caught up to God...it speaks of Jesus' ascension into heaven (Lk.24:51; Acts1:9-11). This is the same word used for the rapture of the church in 1Thes.4:17; in 2 Cor.12:2,4 for Paul's sneak-preview of glory; and again in Acts 8:39 when Philip was miraculously transported after baptizing the Ethiopian eunuch!

Since Satan failed in his previous historical attempts to destroy the Messiah and prevent His coming Kingdom, in verse six he is again seen turning his murderous attention to Israel, where he will seek to exterminate all Jews during the last 42 months of the Tribulation (Dan.9:27); Mt.24:15-21). Though many will die, God will preserve a believing remnant of Israel to enter the Earthly Kingdom of Christ (Dan.12:1; Rom.11:26).

(4)   Tribulation Realities: War in Heaven

(12:7-12) "And there was war in heaven..." This battle between a holy angel and an unholy angel will undoubtedly occur during the mid to final days of the Tribulation (perhaps just before the bowl judgments) and will neither be seen nor experienced by those on earth. We are being reassured here that good will always prevail, even though we may not always see it!

(a) *The contenders (7) "Michael and his angels fought against the dragon, and the dragon fought and his angels."* Interestingly, Jude 9 records an earlier conflict between these two angelic leaders. Take time to read it. Here, the former archangel, Lucifer, now fallen and bent on destroying the magnificent Michael, calls forth his army of demons to do battle against Michael and his angels.

(b) **The consequences (8-12)** At the very outset, in verse 8, we are told that the dragon *"prevailed not, neither was their place found any more in heaven."* There are cataclysmic consequences, both to planet earth and to heaven.

{1} **Consequences related to earth (8-9, 12b)** With *"the great dragon...that old serpent called the Devil and Satan"* being ejected from heaven along with all his fallen angels (demons), this crafty "accuser of the brethren" will wage his final warfare on earth, and it won't be pretty! He will be desperate for destruction, because he will know that his time of defeat and confinement is short.

An important reminder: Some teach that Satan is currently bound as the Church prepares the world for Christ's return. Nothing could be further from the truth! The deceiver of men is indeed alive and well on planet earth. A casual reading of any newspaper or watching the TV news makes it clear that evil forces and actions go beyond the sin nature of man!

{2}**Consequences related to heaven (10-12a)** John hears a heavenly voice declaring *"salvation and strength and the kingdom of our God and the power of His Christ."* The reason for this glorious declaration is twofold: First, it is because *"the accuser of our brethren is cast down."* And second, it is because the saints *"overcome him by the blood of the Lamb, and by the word of their testimony; and they loved not* *their lives unto the death."* <u>Question</u>: Are you an over comer by the blood of the Lamb and by the word of your testimony? Are you also willing to die for Christ?

(5) Tribulation Realities: The Persecuted Woman (12:13-17) Realizing his influence in the heavens is over, Satan will, during the final days of the Tribulation, center his vicious attacks on *"the woman who brought forth the male child"* (Israel).

(a) God's attention to Israel (13-14) Supernatural intervention will help Israel to find asylum during these last 3 ½ years. Her flight *"into the wilderness"* may well be reference to Petra, some 50 miles south of the Dead Sea (read about Petra in your Bible dictionary).

(b) Satan's attacks on Israel (15-17) Hating those *"who have the testimony of Jesus Christ"* (vs.17), Satan will use miraculous powers to try to sweep the fleeing Jews out of the mountain passes. God will intervene and open the earth to swallow the flood. Read Zech.13:8-14:7.

(6)   Tribulation Realities: The Beast Out of the Sea (13:1-10) Two beasts are introduced in this chapter, one from the sea (the antichrist), and one from the earth (the false prophet). The antichrist has been variously (and erroneously) identified as Judas, Nero, the Pope, Hitler, Mussolini, Kissinger, and lately even President Clinton. But none of these fit the profile given by John. His real identity will undoubtedly remain a mystery until after the rapture.

A. His appearance (13:1-2a) – I saw a beast...with seven heads and ten horns...

Here John sees a dreadful, ferocious looking beast [who is a man, v.18] arising from the sea [of Gentile humanity]. Note the family resemblance with the dragon of the abyss in Rev.12:3 – *like father, like son!*

The **ten horns/crowns** represent the ten-nation revived Roman empire, the last Gentile kingdom to oppress Israel (Dan.2:31-43; 7:7-8; 17:12). According to Rev.17:9ff, the **seven heads with blasphemous names** refer to seven mountains or kings/kingdoms which will be the foundation of his rise to power.

The reference to the leopard, bear and lion indicates that this kingdom will blend all the strengths (and weaknesses) of the kingdoms of Greece, Medo-Persia, and Babylon (Dan.7:4-6). This will indeed be a tremendous empire...but still a poor counterfeit of the Kingdom of our Lord and Christ!

B. His Authority (13:2b) This seemingly invincible beast (v.4c) draws his power directly from the dragon. He will be Satan's pawn. The "seat" he is given is a throne/office with global authority and influence.

C. His Assassination (13:3a) Verses 3a, 12, and 14 seem to indicate that someone will attempt to murder the anti-christ with an edged weapon. Though the wound appears to be fatal, he will recover – a counterfeit resurrection! No wonder the whole world will be deceived.

*D. His Adulation (13:3b-4, 8) – and all the world wondered after the beast. And they worshipped the dragon…and they worshipped the beast…*After this lying sign and wonder (2Thes.2:9), the final form of apostate religion takes shape – pure, unadulterated world-wide, Satan worship. Please note that this worship will not be strictly voluntary (13:11f). Men will move from astonishment to adoration of Lucifer, crying out, *Who is like unto the beast?* Read Psalm 2, Psalm 71:19 and Revelation 6:17b; 19:11ff.

E. His Arrogance (13:5-6) Antichrist will violate the third commandment with his contemptuous and gross blasphemies against God. He will rail against:

- God's Name – *His Person*
  - God's Tabernacle – *His Place*
    - God's Servants – *His People*

F. His Aggression (13:7,9-10) Antichrist's exercise of authority, like that of all evil rulers, will be characterized by ruthlessness and great cruelty, by destruction and domination. He will persecute God's people *(make war with the saints and overcome them)* and will tyrannize the world. God's gracious invitation to "hear" in vs.9 will mean certain captivity and even death for those who respond (v.10). There won't be any room for fair-weather saints in that day!

CHRIST	ANTICHRIST
Came from **Above** *John 6:38*	Ascends from **the Pit** *Revelation 11:7*
Came in His **Father's** name *John 5:43*	Comes in his **own** name *John 5:43*
Humbled Himself *Philippians 2:8*	**Exalts** himself *2 Thessalonians 2:4*
Was **Despised** *Isaiah 53:3; Luke 23:18*	Is **admired** *Revelation 13:3, 4*
Exalted *Philippians 2:9*	**Cast down to hell** *Isa. 14:14, 15; Rev. 19:20*
Does His **Father's** will *John 6:38*	Does his **own** will *Daniel 11:36*
Came to **Save** *Luke 19:10*	Comes to **destroy** *Daniel 8:24*
The **Good** Shepherd *John 10:4-5*	The **idol (evil)** Shepherd *Zechariah 11:16, 17*
The **True Vine** *John 15:1*	The **vine of the earth** *Revelation 14:18*
The **Truth** *John 14:6*	The **lie** *2 Thessalonians 2:11*
The **Holy One** *Mark 1:24*	The **lawless one** *2 Thessalonians 2:11*
The **Man of Sorrows** *Isaiah 53:3*	The **man of sin** *2 Thessalonians 2:3*
The **Son of God** *Luke 1:35*	The **son of perdition** 2 *Thessalonians 2:3*

The Personality & Program of the Antichrist

The Bible reveals that the Antichrist will…

1. Appear on the world stage only after the Day of the Lord has begun (2 Thessalonians 2:2).
2. Be the acme of self-exalting, insolence, impiety, and defiance toward God (Dan. 11:36).
3. Possibly be homosexual (Dan. 11:37).
4. Probably be a Gentile – *rising out of the sea* refers to Gentile humanity/nations (Rev. 13:1; 17:5)
5. Disregard his religion heritage (Dan. 11:37)
6. Worship the god of war (Dan. 11:38, 39).
7. Blaspheme God (Dan. 11:36; Rev. 13:4-8), declaring himself to be God (Ezek. 28:6; 2Ths. 2:4).
8. Be personally empowered by Satan (Rev. 13:2-4).
9. Be an intellectual/oratorical (Dan. 8:23; 11:36, 37), political (Rev. 17:11, 12), financial (Rev. 13:16, 17), and military (Rev. 13:4) genius.
10. Rise to power with a deceitful peace program (Dan. 8:25; 9:27).
11. Enjoy brief power, popularity, and prosperity (Dan. 8:24; 11:36; Rev. 13:7).
12. Wield global influence over all nations (Rev. 13:8).
13. Directly rule over a ten-nation union – revived Roman Empire (Dan. 8:20, 24; Rev. 13:1).
14. Establish his headquarters in Jerusalem at the mid-point of the Tribulation (Dan. 11:45).
15. Persecute the saints of God (Rev. 13:7).
16. Ultimately be defeated and cast into the lake of fire along with the Devil and his demons. (Dan. 11:45; Rev. 13:10; 19:20).

(7) Tribulation Realities: The Beast Out of the Land (13:11-18)

Just as the Antichrist will be the great <u>political</u> monarch during the Tribulation, so this second beast will be the great <u>religious</u> monarch. Called *"the false prophet"* in other passages, there are four specific references to this person in Revelation: 13:11-18; 16:13; 19:20; and 20:10. In addition, chapters 17 and 18 relate the influence of this false prophet over the corrupt one-world church (though he is not actually named in these two chapters).

(a) Who He Is: *His Identity (13:11)*

[1] He is from the earth *"And I beheld another beast coming up out of the earth…"* Many believe, though we cannot be dogmatic about it, that his coming out of the earth ("land", possibly Palestine) identifies the second beast as a Jew. In reality, his racial connection is not mentioned.

[2] He has dual strength *"and he had two horns like a lamb"* Called a "false prophet" in 16:13; he will undoubtedly fake religious overtones in the meekness of a lamb. But, the world will soon realize that these two horns (speaking of authority and strength) actually reveal his power as derived from none other than Satan and the Antichrist!

[3] He has dragon-like authority *"and he spoke like a dragon."* Since his authority comes from Satanic influence (the dragon of 12:3 and 9), he will be horribly fearsome and threatening.

(b) What He Does: *His Activities (13:12-18)*

[1] He possesses the power of the Antichrist (vs.12a) *"And he exercises all the power of the first beast before him…"* Literally, he will perform all the satanic power of the Antichrist. This delegated authority will be self-serving and destructive in every way!

[2] He promotes the worship of the Antichrist (vs.12b) *"and causes the earth and those who dwell on it to worship the first beast…"* Using all his power on behalf of the Antichrist, in imitation of the Holy Spirit Who promotes the worship of the Christ; he will demand all humanity to turn their devotion and worship to the Antichrist.

[3] He produces the miracles of the Antichrist (vss.13-18) *"And he doeth great wonders…"* (Literally, "great signs")

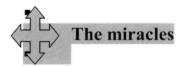 **The miracles**

[1] Invasion of fire from heaven (vs.13) *"…he makes fire come down from heaven on the earth in the sight of men."* This may be an attempt to imitate Pentecost (Acts 2:3) or the fire out of the mouths of two witnesses (Rev.11:5).

[2] Infusion of life in the image of the beast (vs.15) *"And he has power to give life unto the image of the beast"* **Verse** 14 speaks of this huge "image" which the false prophet will build. Obviously, the ability to infuse life into this image will come from Satan himself!

The results

[1] The deception (vs.14) *"And (he) deceiveth them that dwell on the earth by means of those miracles which he had power to do in the sight of the beast..."*

[2] The forced worship (vs.15) Having constructed this image, Satan having given life to it and even the ability to speak, the false prophet will demand the world to recognize this image as god and demand it's worship. The threat will be death for refusal to perform such worship.

An interesting note from Expositors Commentary:

These scholars hold that the extraordinary powers given by Satan to the false prophet do not extend to giving life to that which does not possess life, because this a prerogative of God alone. They say, and Dr. John Walvoord agrees, that the intent of the passage seems to be that the image has only the <u>appearance</u> of life manifested in breathing, but actually it may be no more than a robot.

[3] The mark (vss.16-18) *"And he causes all* (reference to all the unsaved of the Tribulation), *both small and great, rich and poor, free and enslaved, to receive a mark in their right hand, or in their foreheads, and that no man might buy or sell, except he had the mark, or the name of the beast, or the number of his name. Here is wisdom. Let him who has understanding count the number of the beast; for it is the number of a man; and his number is six hundred sixty six."*

<u>A Note on "The Mark":</u> The word "mark" means a brand, engraving, or tattoo, whether visible or invisible, intended to identify a person as a Christ-denier and worshipper of the Antichrist. Such a mark will be necessary to conduct business or to purchase the necessities of life. Here indeed is the satanically enforced control over the human race – either worship the Antichrist or DIE! Verse 17 seems to indicate that this brand may be the Antichrist's name or number.

<u>A Note on the Number 666:</u>   This number emphasizes man's inability to solve his own problems. 7 is God's complete number, while **6** is the number of man, falling short of completeness. In his book The Apocalypse Today Dr. Thomas Torrance states, *"This evil trinity 666 apes the Holy Trinity 777, but always falls short and fails."*

<u>Regarding Rev.13:16-18, Bible Knowledge Commentary states:</u> *"Enforcing his control over the human race and encouraging worship of the beast out of the sea, the second beast (will require) everyone to receive a mark on his right hand or on his forehead...There has been much speculation on the insignia or 'mark' of the beast, but it could be any of several kinds of identification...As there probably have been hundreds of explanations continuing down to the present day, it is obvious that if the number refers to an individual it is not clear to who it refers.*

Probably the best interpretation is that the number six is one less than the perfect number seven, and the threefold repetition of the six would indicate that for all their pretensions to deity, Satan and the two beasts are just creatures and not the Creator. That six is man's number is illustrated in many instances in the Bible, including the fact that man should work six days and rest the seventh...Probably it is best to leave this puzzle unsolved. Probably the safest conclusion is that of Thomas F. Torrance, "This evil trinity 666 apes the Holy Trinity 777, but always fall short and fails."

Chapter 13 introduces two of the main characters of Revelation; The beast out of the sea, the world dictator; and the beast out of the earth..."

(8) Tribulation Realities: The Lamb and the 144,000 (14:1-5)

Chapters 13 and 14 stand in bold contrast, the dark gloom of the rise and rule of the antichrist on the earth is dispelled by this triumphant vision of the Lamb, His saints and His harvest. Dr. Strauss' notes are helpful in placing this portion in proper context:

"In chapter 14 there is a series of seven separate visions, each complete in itself. They are disconnected pictures, however, and are not intended to [be chronological]. By now you...have observed that from time to time the Holy Spirit sets forth in outline a panoramic view of things to come, and...later fills in the details. Chronologically, the events in chapter 15 and 16

occur before the visions of 14. For example, 14:8 [we see] the judgment of Babylon, but her actual doom is described under the seventh bowl judgment 16:17-21...chapter 14 is like a table of contents. It takes the reader back to the beginning of the tribulation week and...forward to the end of the week."

a. An <u>Exalted</u> Company (14:1) – "And I looked, and, Lo, a Lamb stood on the Mount Zion, and with Him, an hundred forty and four thousand..."

128

This Lamb can be no other than the Messiah of Israel, the Lord Jesus Christ (Jn.1:29,24), who now appears to *rectify* all wrong. In 5:6 the Lamb was *crucified*; in 5:8-13 He is *glorified* and worshipped; in 6:1,16 He is *justified* in opening the seals; in 7:9-17 He is *magnified*. Halleluiah! Behold the Lamb!

Mount Zion identifies the site of His appearing as Jerusalem's Temple Mount always seen in connection with the 2nd Advent of Messiah and the establishment of His earthly rule (Zech.14:4, Ps.2:6; 2 Sam.5:7; Ps.48:2; Isa.24:23). It ***does not*** refer to the "heavenly Jerusalem" of Hebrews 12:22.

John has already introduced us to the 144,000 from the 12 tribes of Israel (Rev.7:1ff) who are sealed and protected from harm throughout the Great Tribulation. Notice – not one has been lost! 144,000 Jewish evangelists will be sealed by God at the beginning of Daniel's seventieth week and 144,000 will still be standing at the end of those seven years when Jesus returns to Mt. Zion to initiate His millennial kingdom.

*"In chapter 7:3 we are told that they are sealed in their foreheads. Now we are told what that seal is…**having His***

***Father's name written in their foreheads.** This company is clearly identified with Jesus Christ and the Father. It seems that the seal is visible to the eye, not the invisible seal of the Holy Spirit, as is the case with Christians today (Eph.1:3; 4:30)." (*Strauss, The Book of Revelation, pg. 259)

b. An Exultant Company (14:2-3a) – "And I heard a voice from heaven…And they sung as it were a new song before the throne…" The exalted company will be exulting in the triumph of the Lamb. What a glorious scene! What transcendent music! It seems clear to me that the Lord Jesus Himself (***the voice of many waters***…cf. 1:15; 19:6) will be leading his beloved ones in a concert of joy accompanied by an orchestra of harps. Carnegie Hall – *step aside!*

Isn't it wonderful to know that our God is a God of joy, of song, of music, of delight? Here the Lamb appears on the stage of John's vision and instantly there is music! Isn't this a picture of what happens in every person's heart when Jesus enters? Oh yes, dear ones, when Jesus enters a heart, He brings joy, He brings a song:

> *I have a song that Jesus gave me,*
> *It was sent from heaven above,*
> *There never was a sweeter melody,*
> *It's a melody of love...*

c. An <u>Exclusive</u> Company (14:3b) – *"...and no man could learn that song but the 144,000..."*

This song will belong to these heroes alone, personally dedicated to them by the Lord Jesus Himself. What an honor! Their trials will be unique, so will be the words of this triumphant anthem.

d. An <u>Exemplary</u> Company (14:4-5)

Five exemplary qualities set these saints apart:

{1} In Their Conduct – "These are they which were not defiled...for they are virgins." This is not just a figurative expression for holiness. Phillips says,

"These witnesses have separated themselves...in a practical, purposeful way from the Babylonish, worldly religious system of the Beast, [which] will have at its base a vile immo-

rality that will openly pander to every lust… With the man of sin enthroned, lust will be applauded…as an act of worship [like] the ancient Canaanites."

There's a need for this kind of separation today!

{2} In Their Consecration – "These are they which follow the Lamb wherever he goes." Now, here is the key for saints of every age and situation! No matter how dark the clouds, no matter how heavy the burden, no matter how severe the test, if only we would *follow the Lamb* *wherever* he takes us!

{3} In Their Calling – "These were redeemed…first fruits unto God and to the Lamb." First fruits are the initial ingathering that anticipates a much greater harvest later (1Cor. 16:15). These holy ones are indeed "set apart" unto Jesus for His special purpose in the 70th week of Daniel.

{4} In Their Conversation – "And in their mouth was found no guile." Literally, "no deceit," in contrast with the deceitful nature of antichrist.

{5} In Their Character – "For they are without fault before the throne of God." Not sinless (Rom.3:23), but above reproach in their testimony and because they will refuse the mark of the beast. The only way to be without fault is to belong to the Lamb!

(9) Tribulation Realities: The Everlasting Gospel (14:6-7) If there is only one gospel of salvation, *and there is* (1 Cor. 15:1-4; 2 Cor. 11:4; Gal. 1:6), then what is this gospel?

a. The Nature of the Gospel (14:6) As always the "good news" brings eternal life to all who respond in faith:

{1} It is Eternal in its Significance – "Everlasting"

{2} It is Universal in its Scope – "To every nation..."

b. The News of the Gospel (14:7) The Tribulation gospel will also have a threefold emphasis:

{1} It Involves Conviction – FEAR GOD!

{2} It Involves Conversion – GIVE GOD THE GLORY!

{3} It Involves Consecration – WORSHIP THE CREATOR!

(10) Tribulation Realities: The Doom of Babylon (14:8)

Here the fall of Babylon is both determined and declared by God to be a certainty. The apostate one-world religio-political empire of antichrist is doomed to fail. Verse 8 is a preview of chapters 17 and 18.

(11) Tribulation Realities: The Doom of Those Who Worship the Beast (14:9-12)

In his commentary, The Revelation of Jesus Christ, Dr. John Walvoord provides a good overview of the 14th chapter: *"Taken as a whole, chapter 14 of Revelation emphasizes first that the 144,000 of Israel seen at the beginning of the great tribulation will be preserved triumphantly through it. Second, the rest of the chapter is devoted to various pronouncements of divine judgment upon a wicked world, reassuring the saints of that day that, though they may suffer and even be martyred, God's ultimate justice will triumph, the wicked will be judged, and the saints will be rewarded...The implications of the message for today are only too plain. Today is a day of grace; but what is true of the tribulation is also true today, namely, that God will ultimately judge all men. Today, however, the invitation is still open to those who will trust in Christ and who thereby can avail themselves of the grace of God and be saved from entering this awful period which may be impending for this present generation."*

(a) The Plea of the Angel (vs.9) With a loud voice *"the third angel"* gives a strong warning to any who would worship the Antichrist and his image, receiving his mark.

(b) The Punishment of the Lost (vss.10-11) The outpouring of divine wrath expressed here will actually begin with the Trumpet judgments of chapters 8 & 9, will continue through the bowl judgments of chapter 16, and will extend into eternity!

Verse 11 graphically states the eternal nature of God's judgment: *"And the smoke of their torment ascendeth up forever and ever; and they have no rest day nor night..."* It is important to acknowledge that God's Word not only assures believers of His love, mercy, and grace, but that it also makes absolute statements regarding His wrath on those who reject Christ!

(c) The Patience of the Faithful (vs.12) *"Here is the patience of the saints; here are they that keep the commandments of God and the faith of Jesus Christ."* Christians who suffer during the Tribulation will be encouraged to stand fast with endurance, remembering the terrible fate of those who receive the mark of the beast.

(12) Tribulation Realities: The Blessedness of Those Who Die in Christ (14:13)

John now hears a voice from heaven telling him to reassure those who are martyred, "Blessed are the dead who die in the Lord from henceforth…: All praise to God, they will not die in vain! It is good to note that not only do angels speak in this final prophecy of the Bible, but God's voice is authoritatively heard a number of times. Take a moment to review 10:4, 8; 11:12; 14:2; 18:4; & 21:3.

(a) The Voice from Heaven Assuring Eternal Blessedness to Believing Martyrs (13a) Without a doubt, it is better by far to die at the cruel hand of the antichrist than to receive favor as his worshipper!

(b) The Voice of the Spirit Assuring Eternal Rest to Believing Martyrs (13b) While Hebrews 4 promotes a "faith-rest" life for Christians who are living (as Jesus offered in Matt. 11:28 and Peter speaks of in 1 Pet.4:14), here the Holy Spirit promises eternal rest for these Tribulation martyrs. Incidentally, this is the second of a number of "Blesseds" (beatitudes) in Revelation (see 1:3; 16:15; 19:9; 20:6; 22:7; & 22:14)

(c) The Voice of the Spirit Assuring Eternal Rewards to Believing Martyrs (13c) The faithful works of these believers refer to their standing firmly for the truth even to the point of being put to death! Do you and I have these kinds of "works"?

(13) Tribulation Realities: The Wrath of God on Earth (14:14-20) Here we are given to see God's <u>Agents</u> in bringing judgment to planet earth, as well as the intense <u>agony</u> that will occur among those who are to be judged.

(a) The Agents of Divine Judgment. (Vss. 14-15) Having received a vision of the fall of Babylon (vs.8) and of the doom of those who worship the beast (vss.9-

12), John is now given a graphic fore view of Armageddon, when the earth will be reaped with the sharp sickle of divine judgment.

[1] The Son of Man – Christ (14) John is given to see Christ sitting on cloud, *"having on His head of golden crown* (the victor's crown as coming King, including His glorious and royal dignity!) *and in His hand a sharp sickle* (as the Agent of judgment)".

[2] Three Angels (15a, 17a, 18a) Notice three-fold term *"another angel"* in these verses. As God's agents of judgment, they are viewed as yielding authority to Christ in thrusting in His sickle of judgment on unrepentant man. Jesus speaks of this time in Matthew 13:39 – *"The harvest is the end of the age; and the reapers are the angels."*

(b) The Agony of Divine Judgment (vss.16-20) *"And He that sat on the cloud thrust in His sickle, and the earth was reaped."* In these verses John continues to state the fact of coming judgment, but he emphasizes both the just reason for God's wrath and the graphic result of His wrath!

[1] The <u>Reason</u> for Judgment: The moral rottenness of the world (16-18) As our Lord is seen thrusting in His sickle, *"the earth was reaped",* revealing the destructive ravage to be inflicted by God at the close of the Great Tribulation. The angel entreats Him to *"thrust in thy sickle, and gather the clusters of the vine of the earth, for her grapes are* *fully ripe.* " This reveals the moral rotten and corrupt condition of man at this time.

[2] The <u>Result</u> of Judgment: Blood from the winepress of God's wrath (19-20) Take a moment to compare Isaiah 63:1-6, where the massive carnage of the Battle of Armageddon is prophetically declared. In verse 20 the blood is seen to flow some 182 miles as deep as 5 feet *("unto the horse bridles").*

Another passage to compare is Rev.19:17-19, where God calls the birds of the air to clean up the horrible death scene of the Middle east. 1st century historian Josephus relates that, in A.D. 70, buckets of the blood of the dead were used to douse the fires set by Titus in his invading Jerusalem (graphic example).

D. Vision of the Seven Bowl Judgments (15:1-16:21)
Let's review our broad outline of Revelation thus far:
Introduction, 1:1-8
    I. Vision of Christ, 1:9-20
    II. Vision of the Churches, 2:1-3:22
    III. Vision of the Consummation, 4:1-22:5
        A. Prologue: A Throne, A Scroll, and A Lamb (4:1-5:14)
        B. Vision of 7 Seal Judgments (6:1-8:1)
        C. Vision of 7 Trumpet Judgments (8:2 - 11:19)
        D. Vision of 7 Bowl Judgments

1. Preparation for the Seven Final Plagues (15:1-8)

In chapter 15 John receives a vision of the *seven angels of God*, while chapter 16 is his vision of the *severe anger of God.* Here we are given to see the consummation of divinely ordered events leading up to the second advent of Christ. Chapter 15 reveals what John <u>sees</u> and what he <u>hears</u>:

a. What John Sees (15:1-2a, 5-8)

(1) He sees seven angels (vss.1-2a, 6-7)

(a) **Their assignment (1, 7)** – *To pour out God's final judgment.* The *"sign"* John sees in verse 1 is the result of the 7th Trumpet sounding in 11:15. It is *"great and marvelous"* because it represents the full blast of God's judgment on earth just preceding Christ's glorious earthly reign.

"Marvelous" means anything that causes terror and amazement, because it is beyond human comprehension!

(b) **Their appearance (6) "clothed in pure and white linen, and having their breasts girded with golden girdles"** (an amazing sight to John!)

(2) **He sees a sea of fire and glass, where the victors stand (vs.2a)** Those who **"had gotten the victory over the beast"** are the martyred Tribulation saints. What a lesson! Those who are willing to suffer for Christ are always the winners! Read Matt. 5:10-12; 2 Tim. 2:11-12; 1 Pet. 1:3-7

(3) **He sees a smoke-filled temple (vs.5,8)** John understands that this smoke is from the glory of God and *"from His power"*. Smoke is symbolic in Scripture of judgment (Ex. 19:18; Isa. 6:4).

(a) **The entrance to the Holy of Holies is opened (5),** allowing the angels with the 7 final judgments to come out (verse 6).

(b) The temple itself is closed to all until the bowl judgments are completed (8).

b. What John Hears (15:2b-4)

(1) He hears the singers *"having the harps of God"* **(vs.2b)** Again, these rejoicing victors are the martyred Tribulation saints.

(2) He hears them singing *"the song of Moses…and the song of the Lamb"* **(vss.3-4)** "The Song of Moses" (Ex.15:1-21) expresses praise to God for His salvation and deliverance of Israel, while "The Song of the Lamb" (possibly Psalm 22) expresses Christ's redemption of sinners through the sacrifice of Calvary. Ryrie suggests that the substance of both songs is the mighty works of God in which He is seen as almighty; as righteous and true; as the King of nations (not "saints" as in KJV); as holy, requiring men to fear and glorify Him; and as the One to be worshipped in His Millennial reign.

Consider this comparison of the two songs:
[1] The Song of Moses – sung at the Red Sea
   The Song of the Lamb –at the Crystal Sea
[2] The Song of Moses – a song of triumph over Egypt.
   The Song of the Lamb – a song of triumph over Babylon.
[3] The song of Moses – Tells how God brought His people out
   The Song of the Lamb – Tells how God brought His people in.
[4] The Song of Moses – The *first* song in Scripture.
   The song of the Lamb – The *last* song in Scripture.
[5] The song of Moses – Commemorates the defeat of Pharaoh.
   The Song of the Lamb – Commemorates the defeat of Antichrist

[6] The Song of Moses and the Song of the Lamb are both sung by a gloriously redeemed people.

2. The First Bowl: *Putrefying Sores on the Unsaved (16:1-2)*

The word 'bowl' or 'vial' was familiar to the culture of John's day. It referred to shallow bowls used in temple worship; such a bowl received the blood of sacrificial animals, required as judgment due to sin. Thus, the *"voice out of the temple saying to the seven angels, Go your ways, and pour out the bowls of the wrath of God upon the earth." (vs.1)*

A Review of the chart below will show these bowl judgments to occur at the very end of the seven year Tribulation:

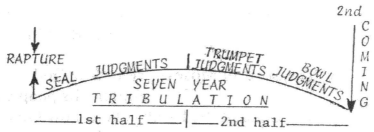

Also, notice similar areas of judgments seen in the trumpet and bowl judgments:

TRUMPETS	AREA of JUDGMENT	BOWLS
8:1-7	The Earth	16:1-2
8:8-9	The Sea	16:3
8:10-11	The Rivers	16:4-7
8:12-13	The Heavens	16:8-9
9:1-12	Torment on Mankind	16:10-11
9:13-21	Armies & Euphrates	16:12-16
11:15-19	God's Wrath on Nations	16:17-21

In Comparing these, notice that the bowl judgments are far more severe and rapid.

Vs.2 *"And the first went, and poured out his bowl upon the earth, and there fell a noisome and grievous sore upon the men who had the mark of the beast…"*

<u>Noisome</u> = that which is injurious and destructive (foul).

<u>Grievous</u> = painful, annoying.

<u>Sore</u> = a deep, putrefying, incurable abscess, probably cancerous leprosy. This is the same word in the LXX (Greek version of the Old Testament) used of the boils with which God smote the Egyptians in Exodus 9:10-11.

The beginning of the final series of judgments reminds us of God's warning in Rev. 14:9-11, that those who worship the beast *"shall drink of the wine of the wrath of God."*

3. The Second Bowl: *Death of All Sea Creatures (16:3) "And the second angel poured out his bowl upon the sea, and it became like the blood of a dead man; and every living soul died in the sea."*

The Greek text provides a more accurate and graphic rendering: *"…it became blood as of a dead man…"* The salt-water seas of the world will literally become blood, corresponding in appearance and in sickening smell to that of a dead person!

Review the 2nd trumpet judgment (8:9), where 1/3 of all sea creatures will die. Here, all sea creatures will die in the unimaginable stench!

4. The Third Bowl: *Fresh Waters Become Blood (16:47*

a. The Judgment of God described (vs.4) *"And the third angel poured out his bowl upon the rivers and fountain of waters, and they became blood."*

Following the pattern of the third trumpet judgment (8:10-11), all of the world's fresh waters (lakes, streams, and rivers) will become blood. As the saying goes, "What goes around comes around" …the unalterable law of retribution!

b. The Justice of God Declared (vss.5-7)

Here is the clear revelation of the absolute right of the eternal God to bring wrath down on the unsaved. Not only have they rejected Jesus Christ, they have, beginning with righteous Abel in Genesis 4, *"shed the blood of saints and prophets".* Verse 6 states, *"Thou hast given them blood to drink, for they are worthy."* And, in verse 7, another angel shouts, *"Even so, Lord God Almighty, true and righteous are Thy judgments".*

5. The Fourth Bowl: Men Scorched with Fire (16:8-9) *"And the fourth angel poured out his bowl upon the sun, and power was given unto him to scorch men with fire."* Compare Malachi 4:1-2, which declares this horrible judgment on the unsaved (also, see Jesus' statement in Luke 21:25)

How tragic that, instead of causing people to turn in repentance to God, they *will "blaspheme the name of God"*, refusing to turn from their evil deeds! During this darkest hour in history, when the world will choose the Antichrist and his False Prophet to follow, they will have no power to direct creation…ONLY GOD *"has power over these plagues."*

6. The Fifth Bowl: The Beast's Kingdom Turned to Darkness (16:10-11) *"And the fifth angel poured out his vial upon the seat [throne] of the beast; and his kingdom was full* *of darkness; and they gnawed their tongues for pain."* Compare this judgment with the Fourth Trumpet Judgment, when the light of the sun, moon and stars were darkened by one-third (Rev. 8:12-13). The fifth plague comes on the "throne" of the Beast, the "seat" of his authority and power. Where will his throne be? This may refer to Jerusalem, his headquarters for the world-wide worship of his image (Rev. 13), or, as indicated in the remainder of the verse, <u>it is a reference to the entire sphere of his influence,</u> *and his kingdom was full of darkness.* Here we should go back and read Exodus 10:21 and the plague of darkness God sent against Pharaoh. "*And the Lord said unto Moses, Stretch out thine hand toward heaven, that there may be darkness over the land of Egypt, even darkness that may be felt…and there was a thick darkness in all the land of Egypt three days. They saw not one another, neither rose any from his place for three days: but all the children of Israel had light in their dwellings."*

<u>The first</u> result of this judgment <u>is a fearful agony</u> throughout the global empire of the antichrist. *They gnawed their tongues* literally means to chew their tongues because of excruciating, intolerable pain. Imagine, a darkness so intense that it can be felt (probably both physically and psychologically)! After all, didn't Jesus associate darkness and torment when he spoke of the eternal suffering of the lost in hell? *But [they] shall be cast out into outer darkness: there shall be weeping and gnashing of teeth* (Mat. 8:12; 22:13; 24:51; 25:30; Rev. 9:2 with 14:10-11). If this isn't a reason to get saved today, I don't know what is!

<u>The second result is a frightening arrogance</u> demonstrated by mankind's evil use of their tongues (Jam. 3:5-6); *[They] blasphemed the God of heaven because of their pains and their sores, and repented not of their deeds.* This familiar

theme (Rev. 2:21; 9:20-21) demonstrates the horrible hardness of men's hearts when they reject the truth and exchange it for the lie (cf. Rom. 1:18-32).

BLASPHEMY!
"To speak profanely of or to God or sacred things; to curse ridicule, to slander."

Lev. 24:11-16 *Punishable by Death*
Rev. 2:9 *...the source of blasphemy*
   Satan's Synagogue
13:1 / 17:3 *...the names of blasphemy*
   Claims to Divinity?
13:5 *...the method of blasphemy*
   Great Swelling Words
   13:6 ...the targets of blasphemy
   God's Person, Place, People
16:9 *...the hardness of blasphemy*
   Refusing to Glorify God
16:11 / 21 *...the excuse of blasphemy*
   Refusing to Repent of Works

Walvoord writes, "When wicked men are confronted with the power of God, they do not easily come to the place of repentance, but instead enlarge their rebellion against God." Each new revelation of God's power merely hardened Pharaoh's heart further! As it was then, so it will be – and even more so – at the End. [Note the contrast with a righteous man's response to suffering in Job 2:7-10.]

7. The Sixth Bowl: Euphrates River Dried Up (16:12-16)

Together with the Sixth Trumpet judgment in 9:13-21, we have a full picture of the hordes from the East (200 million) moving across the dried up Euphrates as part of the Campaign of Armageddon (Read Dan. 11:44 in its context; also Isa.11:15 and Zech. 10:11).

Verses 13-14 describe the leaders of Satan's end-times "signs and wonders" movement as *three unclean spirits...like frogs!* These will be demons sent by Satan to deceive world rulers with counterfeit miracles (cf. 2 Thes.2:3-9; Rev.11:3-6). Remember beloved, not all "signs & wonders" are from God!

Verse 15 provides God's warning of swift destruction that will come upon the unsaved. Verse 16 reminds us that it is God who is ultimately in control of all these events, not Satan!

ARMAGEDDON

"(Gr. Armageddon) (Rev.16:16) Strong's #717: This Greek term, which appears only here in the New Testament, appears to be derived from the word *har*, which means a mountain, and the word *Megiddo*, a name of a city in Manasseh. In this area, God overthrew the Canaanite kings by miraculously aiding Deborah and Barak (Jud.4).

Josiah, the ally of Babylon, was also defeated and slain here.

The name Megiddo comes from a Hebrew root meaning to 'cut off' thus means 'slaughter' (see Joel 3:2, 12, 14). Just the mention of the famous battlefield of Armageddon to a Jew would suggest a horrific slaughter.

(Nelson Study Bible notes, pg. 2190)

8. The Seventh Bowl: History's Greatest Earthquake (16:17-21) (Cf. Rev. 11:15-19 and Zech. 14:4)

It is done, is literally, "It has come to pass" or "It is time!" and refers to the climatic outpouring of Divine Judgment on the earth. By this time, at least 2/3's of humanity will be dead! That's terrible, you say. No, that's merciful, because none deserve to live!

This bowl is poured out "into the air" (vs.17), the present sphere of Satan's activity (Eh.2:2). God's heavenly Drano will finally flush evil once and for all!

The **great earthquake** (vs.18-21) will be the worst natural catastrophe in all of history (Zech.14:1-7 tells us that this will be concurrent with 2nd Advent of Christ and Armageddon). The results:

1. The Mount of Olives will be split. Providing an escape route for the believing remnant of Jews (Zech.4:4-5).

2. The sky will be darkened (Zech. 14:6).

3. Jerusalem "that great city" will be divided into three parts [*but not partitioned with the Palestinian!*] (Rev.11:2. 8; 16:19).
4. Major cities will be destroyed (16:19).
5. Mountains and Islands will be removed (16:20)!
6. 100 pound hailstones will cause great destruction and blasphemy (16:21).

FOURTH PARENTHETIC SECTION (17:1-19:10)

1. Destruction of Ecclesiastical Babylon (17:1-18)

2. Destruction of Commercial Babylon (18:1-24)

3. Heavenly Scene of Praise to God (19:1-6)

4. Marriage of the Lamb (19:7-10)

Once again, after the vivid description of the seven bowl judgments in Chapter 16, which will occur at the very end of the Tribulation, John receives visions of events which will occur during the first half of the Tribulation (chapters 17 and 18). Following these chapters, 19:1-10 moves us back to a heavenly scene of rejoicing over the destruction of the corrupt Babylonish religion and of rejoicing over the marriage of Christ to His Bride, the Church.

1. Destruction of Ecclesiastical Babylon (17:1-18)

Dr. John Walvoord, in his commentary on Revelation, writes: *"The Book of Revelation was written in the order in which the truth was revealed to John, but the events described are not necessarily in chronological order. This is especially true of revelation 17, which probably (will occur) during the first half of the last seven years (of the Tribulation). Much confusion is manifested in interpretations of chapters 17-18, and there is obscurity in the revelation itself. Probably the best solution is to regard chapter 17 as the destruction of ecclesiastical Babylon, or Babylon as a religion, and chapter 18, the destruction of Babylon as a city and as an empire."*

a. The Corrupt Harlot (vss.1-6) – One of the seven "bowl" angels of chapter 16 speaks to John and says, ***"Come here and I will show thee the judgment of the great harlot that sitteth upon many waters."***

Here is revealed in symbolic form the Tribulation church in all her satanically inspired glory! We believe this corrupt *"one world church"* will exist only during the first half of Tribulation and will consist of the <u>corrupt elements</u> of Christendom as suggested in the following chart:

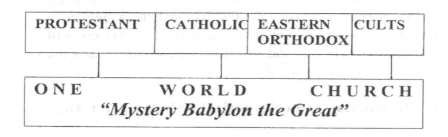

PROTESTANT	CATHOLIC	EASTERN ORTHODOX	CULTS

O N E   W O R L D   C H U R C H
"Mystery Babylon the Great"

(1) The Harlot's *Unlimited* Power (1-2)
The reference in verse to **"many waters"** points to the many Gentile nations that will come under the control of this filthy religious system. Verse 2 States that ***"the kings of***

the earth have committed fornication" (both spiritual and physical) with her. "Fornication" means sexual perversion of a wide variety. The Greek is *porneia,* from which we get the word pornography. How sick and degrading is the thought that such would occur in a religious system!

(2) The Harlot's Unequaled Position (vs.3) *"I saw a woman sit upon a scarlet-colored beast, full of names of blasphemy, having seven heads and ten horns."* This "beast" is undoubtedly the same as named in 13:1, the Antichrist himself, the "man of sin" in 2 Thes.2:3. The woman is the corrupt one-world church of the Tribulation, and she is seen here being supported by the Antichrist and his evil political empire. Obviously, this political sway will take place early in the Tribulation period, because verse 16 reveals the harlot (Tribulation church) being destroyed by those under Antichrist's control.

The *"seven heads"* (see 13:1) refer either to seven mountains (17:9), perhaps the 7-hilled city of Rome, or to successive forms of government during the Tribulation. The *"ten horns"* are kings who will reign simultaneously under Antichrist's control (see17:12).

(3) The Harlot's *Unconfined Prosperity (vs.4a)* *"And the woman was arrayed in purple and scarlet color…"* (purple speaks of the trappings of ecclesiastical pomp, indicating world-wide royalty of the Tribulation church. Scarlet depicts her sinful character, as well as her cruel slaughtering of God's people (see vs. 6).

"and bedecked with gold and precious stones and pearls…" The wicked church's outward display of wealth and beauty, while being inwardly and spiritually bankrupt!

(4) The Harlot's *ungodly* Pursuits (vss.4b-5)
This apostate religious system is seen *"having a golden cup in her hand, full of abominations and filthiness of her fornication"*. Walvoord makes a fitting statement of this passage: *"The Word of God does not spare words in describing the utter filthiness of this adulterous relationship in the sight of God. Few crimes in Scripture are spoken of in more unsparing terms than the crime of spiritual adultery of which this woman is the epitome. As alliance with the world and showy pomp increase, so spiritual truth and purity decline."*

"And upon her forehead was written, MYSTERY BABYLON THE GREAT, THE MOTHER OF HARLOTS AND ABOMINATIONS OF THE

EARTH." Here, the woman corresponds religiously to what Babylon always was religiously – pagan and corrupt! As a comparison of God's hatred of such false profession, read His warning to the church at Thyatira in Rev. 2:22-23.

(5) The Harlot's *Unrelenting Persecutions (vs.6)*
"And I saw the woman drunk with the blood of the saints and with the blood of the martyrs of Jesus." No wonder John "wondered" with shocked amazement! With the true Church having been taken up to heaven, this counterfeit church of the Tribulation will actually engage in slaughtering followers of the Lord Jesus! This world-wide persecution will surpass anything known to man. Compare the 6th Seal judgment of Rev. 6:9-11.

b. The Carrying Beast – *Political Babylon* (vss.7-18)
The woman riding on the scarlet – colored beast is quite a spectacle *(Mystery Babylon the Great, the bride of Antichrist, is an apostate, syncretistic, world-wide, religious system)*. John

was astounded by her gaudy attire, gross idolatry, and great antagonism toward the saints of God. But now, the identity of the beast itself is revealed.

(1) The Source & Destiny of the Beast (vss. 7-8a) ... *I will tell you the mystery...of the beast that carries her.* The key to the future power of the woman will be her political alliance with Satan's revived Roman Empire. It is interesting that the word for *carry* means literally "to carry as a burden, to carry away, to steal." The political arm of the antichrist's power will exploit religion for Satan's own purposes, but in the end, even the pretense of religion will become a burden (vs.16)!

The phrase, *The beast that...was, and is not; and shall ascend...*used <u>three times</u> in the context (17:8, 11) must be compared with Rev. 1:4,8 and 4:8 *(who is, and who was, and who is to come).* Here the Holy Spirit is exposing the antithesis between the titles/natures of Satan and the Lord Jesus. Perhaps this is another hint at the counterfeit trinity already seen in chapter 13 [*the beast, the false prophet, the dragon*]?

The Satanic <u>source</u> of the beast's power (cf.9:11; 11:7; 13:3) is revealed in the phrase, *shall ascend out of the bottomless pit.* The den of demons – the Abyss – shall energize future Babylon the Great!

The <u>destiny</u> of this great beast is described as *going forth to destruction* (Dan. 2:34, 35; Rev. 20:10). The words of Martin Luther's greatest hymn are fitting reminders of this biblical certainty – that Jesus Christ will triumph in the end:

> "The Prince of Darkness grim, we tremble not for him,
> His rage we can endure, <u>for lo, his doom is sure,</u>
> One little Word shall fell him."

(2) The Surprise & Denial of the Beast-Worshippers (vs.8b) *...and they that dwell on the earth shall* *wonder, whose names were not written in the book of life…*These are the members of the one-world "church" of the antichrist. Their names are on his roster as ones who have received the mark of the beast and have bowed to his image (13:4, 8; 14:10, 11). But their names are not in the Lamb's book (20:11ff)

Shall wonder means "the amazement of a horrible surprise." The grim reality of who they now worship will yet dawn on these who sold their souls. They have exchanged the truth for the lie (Rom. 1:25).

(3) The Seat & Dominion of the Beast (vss.9-13) *The seven heads are seven mountains, on which the woman sitteth.* Dr. Ryrie in his commentary on Revelation (pages 118, 119) writes:

"The seven heads of the Beast are identified as the seven mountains on which the harlot sits. No reasonable doubt can be entertained as to the meaning of these words – the seven hills of Rome. In other words, the center of the harlot's [religious system's] power will be Rome.

As to the identification of the "seven kings" (v.10), there is greater difficulty. Some have interpreted them as a selective list of Roman emperors (since more than five had reigned up to John's time). Others [suggest] that they refer to a selective list of world empires… [but neither view can be asserted dogmatically].

In any case, the Beast that is to come during the Tribulation is definitely said to be the "eighth" in whatever list is meant (v.11), and his power is limited by God and his doom is [declared by God]."

McGee suggests the following in explaining vs. 10:
  1. Julius Caesar –assassinated
  2. Tiberius – poisoned or smothered
  3. Caligula – assassinated
  4. Claudius – poisoned
  5. Nero – committed suicide.

The one is refers to Domitian who was living in John's day, but was later assassinated. *The other is not yet come* refers to the Antichrist who will rule over the revived Roman Empire.

And the ten horns which you saw are ten kings...[who] receive power as kings one hour [for a brief time, cf. Dan.7:25] *with the beast* (vs.12). The "ten horns" and the "ten kings" are one and the same as the vision of the "ten toes" of Daniel 2 and 7:24.

Verse 13 tells us that this 10 nation confederacy will not rule independently, **for they have one mind, and shall give their power and strength to the beast.** They will draw their authority from and pay obeisance to the Antichrist. This power will last only until the end of the Tribulation, when Jesus Christ, the Lamb of God, returns with his saints (19:15).

(4) The Sovereignty of & Devotion to the Lamb (vs.14) *These shall make war with the Lamb, and the Lamb shall overcome them: for He is Lord of lords, and King of kings...*

In their arrogant desperation they will actually attempt to fight with Christ Himself! Both ecclesiastical and political Babylon will be utterly opposed to God and all those who follow Jesus. But here we also see the ultimate triumph of the Lamb leading to the final destruction of the Harlot.

"Along with the Lord will be an army of Old Testament believers, church-age believers, and Tribulation saints, properly identified as called, and chosen and faithful (vs. 14)" according to David Levy writing for Israel My Glory magazine (Feb/Mar 98).

(5) The Scope & Diversity of the Beast's Influence (vs. 15)

Here is the explanation of the waters which support the harlot (vs.1). The Gentile nations of the world will prostitute themselves with the corrupt religious system of the Antichrist. The entire world will be intoxicated by her seductive lures (17:2).

(6) The Sedition & Desolation of the Beast (vss.16-18)
And the ten horns…shall hate the whore, and shall make her desolate and naked, and shall eat her flesh, and burn her with fire. God sovereignly impels Antichrist to turn against his religious whore. The Beast hates the very religious system he has used to consolidate his power. God uses the wrath of men to praise Him and in His time, he will bring an end to the corrupt world church as well as Babylon itself.

"The Seven Heads are Seven Mountains"
(Rev. 17:9)
(Alexander Hislop, *The Two Babylons,* pages 1-3)

There never has been any difficulty in…identifying the woman *sitting on the seven mountains.* And having on her forehead the name written, *Mystery, Babylon the Great,* with the Roman apostasy. "No other city in the world has ever been celebrated, as the city of Rome has, for its situation on seven hills. Pagan poets and orators…have [called] it 'the seven-hilled city.'"

Virgil refers to it; "Rome [is] the most beautiful city in the world and alone has surrounded for herself seven heights with a wall." **Propertius** speaks of it as: "The lofty city on seven hills, which governs the whole world." [cf. Rev. 17:18] **Horace** spoke of Rome when he wrote, "The gods who have set their affections on the seven hills." **Martial**, in like manner, speaks of "the seven dominating mountains."

To some it will appear a very startling position…that the Church which has its seat and headquarters on the Seven Hills of Rome might most appropriately be called "[Spiritual] Babylon." But let the reader judge for himself whether I do not bring ample evidence to substantiate my position.

BABYLON & ROME

(Clarence Larkin, *The Book of Revelation,* pages 151, 152)

Babel was the seat of the first great Apostasy. Here the "Babylonian Cult" [originated and remained] the seat of Satan until the fall of the Babylonian/Persian Empires, when he shifted his Capital to Pergamos (Rev. 2:12, 13).

When Attalus, Pontiff and King of Pergamos, died in 133 BC, he bequeathed the Headship of the Babylonian Priesthood to Rome. When the Eutruscans came to Italy from Lydia, they brought with them the Babylonian religion and rites [and] set up a Pontiff...head of the Priesthood. Later the Romans accepted this Pontiff as their civil ruler.

Julius Caesar was made Pontiff of the Eutruscan Order in 74 BC, [and later] "Supreme Pontiff" of the "Babylonian Order," [and] heir to the rights and titles of Attalus. Thus the first Roman Emperor became the Head of the Babylonian Priesthood, and Rome the successor to Babylon.

The Emperors of Rome continued [in] the office of Supreme Pontiff until AD 376, when Gratian...refused it. The Bishop of the Church of Rome, Damasus, was elected to the position. So in AD 378 the Head of the Babylonian Order became the Ruler of the Roman Church. Thus Satan united Rome and Babylon in One Religious System.

Soon...the rites of Babylon began to come to the front. The worship of the Virgin Mary...in 381 [and] the observance of Easter (Ishtar, the Babylonian Queen of Heaven) began in 519.

2. Destruction of Commercial Babylon (18:1-24

In understanding the distinction between the religious and politico-commercial aspects of Babylon, Ryrie's commentary makes a fitting comment: "Babylon involves a city (certainly Rome and perhaps Babylon on the Euphrates) and a system. The religious aspects of that system was described in the preceding chapter; this chapter concerns other facets of Babylon, chiefly commerce (vs. 3, 7, 9, 11-13, 19). In addition, there is another difference between these two chapters. In chapter 17 it was the beast and his allies who destroyed the harlot Babylon. Here it is God Who destroys this aspect of Babylon (v.8).

a. The Report of God's Judgment (vss. 1-2a)
John states that "after these things" (following what he was given to see in chapter 17) he saw another angel, the same kind as in 17:1, *"having great power"* (literally, authority). Though *"the earth was made bright with his glory"*, this does not mean he was Christ. This angelic being had glorious authority and power, because it was delegated to him by God, and by the greatness of the occasion!

His report is seen in verse 2a, where *"he cried mightily with a strong voice, saying Babylon the great is fallen, is fallen..."* The double emphasis of <u>fallen</u> reveals the terrible judgment to come on the entire Babylonish system of godlessness. Some suggest it points to the <u>double overthrow</u> of chapters' 17 and 18 (religious and commercial Babylon).

b. The <u>*Reasons*</u> for God's Judgment (2b-3)
Three specific reasons are given for the Divine out-pouring of judgment on commercial Babylon:

(1) Demon possession (v.2b)

"Babylon…has become the habitation of demons, and the hold (prison) *of every foul spirit* (Eph. 2:2 and 1 John 4:6 use "spirit" to refer to Satanic control) *and the cage of every unclean and hateful bird"* (obvious reference to demonic beings).

(2) Depraved promiscuity (v.3a)

Entire nations and heads of state will become intoxicated with the filthy, immoral life-style of Babylon! *"her fornication"* refers to sexual perversion of every conceivable variety.

(3) Detestable profligacy (v.3b)

"The merchants of the earth are grown rich through the abundance of her delicacies". This godless Tribulation culture will be involved in a luxurious and careless ease (meaning of *"delicacies"*), which will make people simple targets of Satan's plan. Little does Satan know that he is being set for destruction!

c. The *Request* in light of God's Judgment (vs.4) The voice John hears is that of God Himself, as he pleads with Tribulation saints not to compromise, but rather to *"come out of her".* To remain in this idolatrous system would result in chastisement from God, the intended warning of the phrase, *"that you receive not of her plagues".* (share her punishment).

For the believer today, there is a relevant and serious application! God calls us to separate ourselves

from an unequal yoke (1 Cor. 6:14) with unbelievers and every form of Satan's world-system (both religious and commercial). Take a moment to read Numbers 16:23-26; Isaiah 48:20; 2 Cor. 6:14-17; and 1 John 2:15-17. God's people are to be pure and uncompromising with every aspect of evil!

d. The Results of God's Judgment (vss.5-8)

These verses reveal both a Divine remembrance and retribution as regards the heinous sins of the Tribulation Babylon. Romans 12:19 provides a stern reminder: "I will repay, saith the Lord".

(1) Remembrance of Babylon's sins (5)

Here indeed is a Divine Law that weaves its way throughout Scripture! *"Her sins have reached unto heaven, and God hath remembered her iniquities."* Be sure your sins will find you out! (Num. 32:23)

(2) Retribution for Babylon's sins (6-8)

Verse 7 reminds us of the sinful pride and luxurious lifestyle of this pagan Tribulation system, while verses 6 and 8 declare God's retribution in bringing her down to total destruction. Indeed, *"Strong is the Lord Who judges her"!* While she will claim to *"sit as a queen"* who will *"see no sorrow"*, her plagues of death, mourning and famine will come *"in one day"*.

Tim LaHaye, in his book <u>Revelation Unveiled</u>, makes a fitting statement: *"Once rebuilt, the great city of Babylon will serve as the seat of Satan, the governmental, religious, and commercial headquarters of the world during the Tribulation. In spite of her splendor and magnitude, this will be the most short-lived of the capitols of the world, for she will be earmarked for destruction by Almighty God."*

e. The <u>Reactions</u> to God's Judgment (vss. 9-20) The kings and merchants on the earth are going to be wailing with sorrow, while the saints in heaven will be worshipping with joy!

(1) Reaction of the kings and merchants of the earth (9-19)

(a) The kings' reaction (9-10) John states here that, following the destruction of religious and commercial

Babylon, the governmental leaders of the world will react in three ways: they will *"bewail her"* (lit. "cry aloud"; "weep"), *"lament for her"* ("beat one's breast as an act of mourning"), and *"stand afar off for fear of her torment"* (because they will have been caught up in Babylon's fornication and luxurious life-style).

(b) The merchants' reaction (11-19) Just as with the kings, all the world's crooked business people *"who were made rich by her"* (v.15*), "shall weep and mourn over her; for no one buyeth their merchandise any more."* The loss of their profitable trade with commercial Babylon *"so great riches are come to nothing"* (v.17) will totally demoralize all those who have been made dishonorably rich.

Verses 12 and 13 list the many items which will come from various parts of the world (take a moment to read of the precious metals and stones, fine fabrics and woods, perfumes and spices, various animal life, and even **slave trade**!) Dr. Walvoord comments: *"The combined picture is one of complete abandonment to the wealth of this world and total disregard of God Who gave it."*

(2) Reaction of the saints of heaven (20) In stark contrast to the weeping of the lost people of the world, God here calls on His people to celebrate the fall of Babylon: *"Rejoice over her, thou heaven, and ye saints, apostles and prophets; for God hath avenged you on her."* (Literal rendering of vs.20)

f. The <u>*Range*</u> of God's Judgment (vss. 21-24)

Now John hears the final stanza of Babylon's funeral dirge (cf. Ezk. 27 for a similar lament over Tyre).
This destruction will be vast, violent and justified. Phillips writes, "One moment, prosperous Babylon stands a queen of cities…the next moment she is gone, forever gone!"

(1) *The violence* of Babylon's fall (21)

Suddenly and unexpectedly the final end comes. A powerful, unnamed angel, perhaps Michael, the prince of Israel *(At that time Michael shall stand up, the great prince who stands watch over the sons of your people...*Dan. 12:1) hurls a gigantic millstone into the sea to illustrate the swift, violent destruction. This is the same imagery used by Jesus for the severe retribution that will befall the wicked in Mt. 18:6.

(2)The *vastness* of Babylon's fall (22-23a)

The refrain, **"No more!"** is repeated six times (the number of man) and declares the finality and totality of the city's ruin. In Jeremiah 25:8-10, Judah was warned of judgment that would come at the hands of Babylon. Now the tables are turned and Babylon will be judged. So much for the pride of Satan – as well as all human pride.

(a) No more music *– And the voice of the harpers,...musicians,...pipers and trumpeters, shall be heard no more at all in thee;* A deafening silence will blanket the city! The party is over! The trumpets will no longer herald the entrance of Antichrist into his palace. Instead, total silence will be the calm that heralds the approach of Christ's return as described in the next chapter! Stay tuned.

(b) No more work *– and no craftsman, of whatever craft he be, shall be found any more in thee; and the sound of a millstone shall be heard no more at all in thee;* All industry will cease. The economic collapse of the Revived Roman Empire will be complete. So much for trusting in the treasures of earth (Prov. 10:2; Jer. 48:7, 8; Lk 12:20-21)!

(c) No more light – *and the light of a candle shall shine no more at all in thee;* God is going to turn out the light on Babylon, my friend. Not even a night-light will be left on! Those who love darkness rather than light will get just what they deserve (Jn.3:18-20, 36)

(d) No more joy – *and the voice of the bridegroom and of the bride shall be heard no more at all in thee:* The joys of life will be replaced by sorrow and anguish of soul for those who have followed Satan. What a contrast between this picture of despair and the hope of the righteous (Rev. 21:1-4).

(3) The *validity* of Babylon's fall (23b-24)

"Politically, Babylon symbolizes prideful rebellion against God…Economically, Babylon symbolizes the pride of wealth and sensuality…Religiously, Babylon symbolizes the mother of idolatrous religion and the worship of Satan." (David Levy)

(a) Babylon's pride – *for thy merchants were the great men of the earth*…Pride before the fall!

(b) Babylon's perversion – *for by thy sorceries [occult arts] were all nations deceived.*

(c) Babylon's persecution – *And in her was found the blood of prophets, and of saints, and of all that were slain upon the earth.* We should never gloat over our enemies, but we will rejoice at God's righteous judgment of evil (Rom. 12:17f).

3. Heavenly Scene of Praise to God (19:1-6)

In the fourth and final parenthetic section (17:1-19:10), we have seen the destruction of Ecclesiastical Babylon in chapter 17; the destruction of Commercial Babylon in chapter 18; and now we come to a preview of things John sees and hears preceding the Second Advent of Jesus Christ. Take a moment to review the overall Outline of Revelation, especially the parenthetic section on page 16 and events following.

The first ten verses of chapter 19 transport us back to heaven where, as so well put by J. Vernon McGee, "The somber gives way to song and from dreary days of judgment to bright days of blessing."

a. The Groups Who Praise Him – Beginning with John's hearing *"a great voice of many people in heaven"*, there are four different groups shouting *"Hallelujah!"*. It is significant that, while this term meaning "Praise the Lord" is repeated 24 times in the Psalms, it is found only four times in the entire New Testament, and they are all found right here in verses 1-6.

(1) *"Many people in heaven"* **(vss.1-3)** As seen in Rev. 7:9-14, they are those who will be saved and martyred during the Tribulation. Their shout of *"Hallelujah"* is for their salvation as well as for God's *"true and righteous judgments"* on ecclesiastical and commercial Babylon, whose eternal punishment is seen is the declaration, *"her smoke rose up forever and ever."* (vs3)

(2) *"The twenty four elders"* **(vs.4)** Who are the Elders? While some think they are the redeemed of all time and others prefer to see them as representative of the Church, they may well be redeemed Israel of the Old Testament (12 Tribes) and the redeemed Church of the New Testament (12 Apostles). See Rev. 4:4, 10.

(3) *"The four living creatures"* **(vs.4)** As seen in Rev. 4:6-8; Ezek. 1:5 and 10:20, these are Angelic beings called Cherubim. In Ezek. 10:20, the prophet says regarding the "living creatures...I knew that they were the Cherubim." From their position at the gate of Eden (Gen. 3:24) and on the Ark of the Covenant (Ex. 25:18-20), as well as before God's throne in Rev. 4:6, they are evidently connected with vindicating the holiness of God against the presumptuous pride of sinful man.

(4) *"A voice out of the throne"* (vs.5) This is probably an unnamed angel and possibly Gabriel the "announcing angel" calling for all who serve God with a holy and awesome fear to *"praise our God"*.

b. The Reasons They Praise Him – Three specific reasons are given in this context:

(1) Because the great harlot has been judged (vs. 2a)

(2) Because He has avenged the blood of those cruelly killed by the great harlot (vs. 2b).

(3) Because the Lord God Omnipotent reigns (vss. 5-6)

As so well put by Tim LaHaye in his book <u>Revelation Unveiled</u>, *"The united song of all those in heaven anticipates the rulership of the Lord God by His Son, Jesus Christ."* Truly, here is the greatest of all **HALLELUJAH CHORUSES!**

4. Marriage of the Lamb (19:7-10)

The announcement of the marriage of the Lamb is made in verse 7. But is this the wife of Jehovah or the Bride of Christ? In 2 Cor. 11:2 Paul declares that the church will be presented to Christ as a chaste virgin.

"Now I am aware of the marriage symbolism in the Old Testament used to express the relationship between God and His people. This is clear in such passages as (Isa. 54:6; Jer. 3:14; Ezk.16; Hos. 2:19-20). [However], the prophesied union between God and Israel is an event to take place on the earth, and must not be confused with the marriage of the Lamb to His

163

Bride, which takes place in Heaven...to fail to distinguish between the two [events] only tends to confuse the whole issue. In [Rev. 19] the Lamb's wife is the Church, not Israel. In Rev. 21:9-10, the Lamb's wife is seen descending out of Heaven as the heavenly Jerusalem, a city used symbolically for the Bride, just as Babylon is used symbolically of the harlot."

(Strauss, The Book of Revelation, pg. 318-319)

a. The Presentation of the Bridegroom (vss. 7,8)

In modern, western culture, the bride is announced at a wedding, but not in this case. Here, the Bridegroom is the center of attention. It's as if the heavenly choir was singing "Here Comes the Bridegroom!" Jesus Christ deserves all the glory!

(1) Rejoice with Him (7a). *Let us be glad and rejoice...***is a command that should read,** *Let us keep on rejoicing. Let us keep on being glad exuberantly!*
Why such joy? "The church is the dearest object in the entire universe to the Lord of glory, for she is His bride. At the moment of conversion we are espoused to the Lord Jesus and receive the "engagement ring," the earnest, of the Holy Spirit. But the wedding has been postponed these many centuries. The glorious bridegroom is in heaven preparing a place for us, and we have His promise that He is coming again. At the beginning of the Apocalypse, the rapture to glory took place. Now the time of the wedding is come." (Phillips, *Exploring Revelation.* Page. 229).

(2) Render honor to Him (7b). *Let us give the glory to Him at once, because the wedding of the Lamb has come...* (Wuest's translation).

(a) His Marriage – This wedding occurs after the Judgment Seat of Christ (see notes pg. 153).
(b) His Wife – is ready and robed.

Her preparation has been completed (Eph. 5:27). Her gown (the pure linen of a holy and fruitful life of service for Christ) stands in stark contrast with the harlot's gaudy attire. (17:4)

b. The Pronouncement of the Banquet (vs.9)

(1) The blessedness of the saints
The Jewish wedding is followed by a supper and a special blessing is pronounced on the friends of the Bridegroom (cf. Jn. 3:29). These are the redeemed of other ages, not the church itself, which is the bride. Perhaps this is when we will meet Joshua and Moses!

(2) The truthfulness of God
This glorious wedding celebration is our present hope- a confident expectation because of the faithfulness of God's word. Halleluiah!

c. The Protest of the Angelic Being (vs. 10)
(1) The terror of holiness – *I fell at his feet to worship him…he said…see thou do it not!* John is in awe of the holy angel, but he is told not to worship a fellow servant. Only God is worthy of worship!

(2) The testimony of Jesus – The purpose of prophecy is to turn our thoughts to Jesus and the title of this book is *the unveiling of Jesus Christ* (1:1)

"His wife hath made herself ready" (Rev. 19:7)
at
The Judgment seat [Bema] of Christ
(a review)

1. Scripture – Rom. 14:10-12; 1 Cor. 3:9-15; 2 Cor. 5:10

2. Definition – In Grecian games, the stadium contained a raised platform, on which the umpire sat and from which the contestants were rewarded. It was called the 'bema' or 'reward seat.' It was never used as a judicial bench.

3. Time – For the Church, after the rapture and before the millennial kingdom of our Lord Jesus Christ (2 Tim. 4:8; 1 Cor. 4:5).

4. Place – In Heaven with Christ (2 Cor. 5:8).

5. The Judge – Christ Jesus Himself (Jn. 5:22).

6. The Subjects – Church age believers only (all the saved from Pentecost to the Rapture). Old Testament saints will be rewarded at the 2nd Coming of Christ (Mt. 25:31-46; Joel 3:1-3; Ezk. 20:33-44).

7. The Purpose of Examination – Not for salvation or sin (Rom. 8:1; Heb. 10:17), but to assay/evaluate our "works," whether they are worthwhile *(gold, silver, precious stones)* or worthless *(wood, hay, stubble)* (1 Cor. 3:10-15; 4:5; Eph. 6:8; Col. 3:25). Our sins were judged once and for all at the cross, but our works will be evaluated to determine our crowns or rewards. But even these crowns will be cast at his feet as praise for His mercy and grace.

Different Judgments in the Bible

1. The Judgment of Christ on the Cross – As our substitute, Jesus bore the sins of the world and paid for them in full. (Jn. 12:31; Heb. 9:26-28). His death fully satisfied the righteous demands of God's judgment against sin, making salvation possible.

2. The Believer's Self-Judgment – In 2 Cor. 11:31-32, Paul describes confession of personal sin as self-judgment. Humbly agreeing with God about our sin (1 Jn. 1:9) avoids Divine discipline (Heb. 12:6f). This is never an excuse to sin (Rom. 6:1-6), but it frees us to serve Christ (Php. 3:12-14).

3. The Judgment Seat of Christ – The "Bema" seat is described in Rom. 14:10-12; 1 Cor. 3:9-15; and 2 Cor. 5:10. After the Rapture of the Church and before the Marriage Supper of the Lamb and the Revelation of Christ's return to rule the earth, the "works" of all Church Age believers will be evaluated for rewards.

4. The Judgment of Survivors of the Tribulation (Gentiles and Jews) – This judgment will determine who will enter into the kingdom of Christ and who will be excluded (Mt. 25:31-46; Joel 3:1-3; Ezek. 20:33-44).

5. Judgment of the Fallen Angels – At the end of history the angels who followed Lucifer will be cast into the Lake of Fire (Mt. 25:41; 1Cor. 6:3; Rev. 20:10).

6. The Great White Throne Judgment – All the unsaved of all the ages will appear before Christ to determine their eternal destiny (Php. 2:9-11; Rev. 20:11-15).

E. Vision of Christ's Second Coming (19:11-21)

As a refresher of the contents of Revelation to this point, here's an abbreviated outline:

Introduction, 1:1-8
I. Vision of the Christ, 1:9-20
II. Vision of the Churches, 2:1-3:22
III. Vision of the Consummation, 4:1-22:5
    A. Prologue: A Throne, A Scroll, and A Lamb, 4:1-5:14
    B. Vision of the Seven Seal Judgments 6:1-8:1 [1ˢᵗ Parenthetic Section, 7:1-17]
    C. Vision of the Seven Trumpet Judgments 8:2-11:19
    [2ⁿᵈ Parenthetic Section, 10:1-11:14]
    [3ʳᵈ Parenthetic Section, 12:1-14:
    D. Vision of the Seven Bowl Judgments 15:1-16:21
    [4ᵗʰ Parenthetic Section, 17:1-19:10]
    E. Vision of Christ's Second Coming 19:11-21

Beginning with chapter 19, God reveals a rapid nine-fold **"countdown to eternity"**, as follows:

- Marriage of the Lamb, 19:7-10
- Manifestation of the King, 19:11-16
- Battle of Armageddon, 19:17-21
- Binding of Satan, 20:1-3
- Christ's Earthly 1,000 Year Reign, 20:4-6
- Brief Loosing of Satan, 20:7-9
- Satan's Doom in the Lake of Fire, 20:10
- Great White Throne Judgment, 20:11-15
- New Heavens and New Earth, 21:1-22:5

In the passage before us, 19:11-21, we are shown specific details of Christ's glorious return to earth and the graphic results of His return.

1. Details of His Return (1911-16)
a. The Announcement of the King of Kings (vs.11)
(1) What John saw (11a) *"And I saw heaven opened and, behold, a white horse…"* What a stark contrast between this white horse and that of 6:2 (Antichrist seeking to counterfeit the true Christ by going forth to conquer on a white horse)!

Though some have attempted to symbolize this "white horse" as a metaphor of purity and power, there is no reason to see it as such. Just as Jesus rode into Jerusalem on a colt in His first coming, so He will ride to earth on a white horse in His second coming!

(2) Who John saw (11b) *"And He that sat upon him was called Faithful and True, and in righteousness He doth judge and make war."* Here is the magnificent and exciting event looked forward to by all the Old Testament prophets and promised by Christ Himself (Matt. 24:27-31; 25:31). Jesus, whose first coming was a Savior, is now seen in His Second Coming as Sovereign. Take a moment to read the above passages in Matthew. Then, compare this with Isaiah 59; 63:1-6; Joel 3:1-2, 14-17; Zeph. 3:8-20; Zech. 14:3-4,9. These and so many other passages make it clear that THE BEST IS YET TO BE!

The descriptions of Christ *as "Faithful and True"* are fitting titles for One Who will judge the nations and establish His righteous reign on earth. He is totally trustworthy in His Person, Program, and Promises (compare Deut. 7:9; 1 Cor. 1:9; 1 Thes. 5:24; Rev. 3:14). And never forget: Even in the matter *of "judgment and war"*, what Christ does is always *"in right-eousness"* (always right) Jer. 10:10; John 14:6.

b. The Appearance of the King of Kings (vss. 12-13)

(1) His attributes (12) *"His eyes were like a flame of fire, and on His head were many crowns..."* By attributes we mean those qualities of perfection which belong to God. His "eyes" declare that his judgment is based upon infinite knowledge, purging and cleansing even as he judges (see Heb. 4:13). The *"many crowns"* reveals Christ's badge of divine royalty, confirming His right to rule.

The *"name written that no man knew, but He Himself"* is not revealed to us. Dr. Harry A. Ironside makes this comment regarding verse 12, as well as the names *"The Word of God"* **(vs13)** and *"King of kings"* **(vs.16)** – The name no man knew in vs. *12 "speaks of His essential glory as the eternal Son, concerning which He declared that 'no man knoweth the Son but the Father'. The second name is 'The Word of God', His incarnation, the Word becomes flesh. And, third, 'King of kings and Lord of lords' speaks of his second advent to reign."*

(2) His apparel (13) *"And He was clothed with vesture dipped in blood..."* This is not a reference to

Christ's sacrificial blood; rather, as confirmed in Isa 63:1-6; Rev. 14:20 and 16:14-16, it is the blood of those judged at the Battle of Armageddon. Especially read Isaiah 63:1-6.

c. The Armies of the King of Kings (vs.14)

Rather than limit these *"armies in heaven"* that will follow Christ on white horses to just the Church (as some do), these armies undoubtedly include <u>all</u> the redeemed from Adam through the Church Age and through the Tribulation. Some even include the host of holy angels.

d. The Avenging of the King of Kings (vss. 15-16) In His triumphant return from heaven to earth Christ will *"smite the nations"* as He *"treads the winepress of the fierceness and wrath of almighty God."* Take a moment to read the great Psalm of His coming to earth in Psalm 2; and also Joel 2:15; Amos 5:16-20; Zephaniah 1:7-9.

This fierce avenging will be accomplished when *"Out of His mouth goeth a sharp sword, that with it He should smite the nations".* Since the Word of God is spoken of as a sword in Ephesians 6:17 and Hebrews 4:12, it seems obvious that the reference is to Christ speaking judgment out of His omnipotent mouth. Theodore Epp fittingly says, "The equipment for this last great battle is strange indeed. The heavenly armies do not fight. The Lord alone is equipped to battle. Only the General Himself is going to fight. He has only the sword of his mouth…All the armies of the earth will be gathered together to fight against the Lord…By His word the Lord Jesus Christ will destroy those who defy Him in this last great battle." No wonder His name is *"King of kings and Lord of lords." (vs.16)!!!*

2. Results of His Return (19:17-21)
Here John paints a vivid picture of the wide-spread slaughter that will occur at the conclusion of the Armageddon campaign (read Rev. 14:14-20; 16:13-16; Joel 3:2-17; Zeph. 1:7-18; Zech. 12:1-9; 14:1-2; Matt. 24:27-28).

a. The Supper of the Great God (vss. 17-19)
McGee writes, "If there is one passage of Scripture which is revolting to read, this is it. You will notice that God included it at the end of His Word to remind us how revolting and nauseating to Him are the deeds of the flesh. Men who live in the flesh will have their flesh destroyed…My friend, it is frightful to rebel against God because He is going to judge you

someday. This scene reveals the heart of man and how dreadful that heart really is." (Thru the Bible, Vol. 5, pg. 1051)

(1) The Carnage (vss.17-18)

(a) The Command Voice. *"And I saw an angel...and he cried with a loud voice, saying to all the fowls...in the midst of heaven, Come and gather yourselves together unto the supper of the great God;"*

The angel's cry is really a command shouted to creation. Its volume indicates something of great significance is about to occur (cf. 6:10; 7:2, 10; 10:3; 14:15; 18:2). There is a stark contrast between this invitation to the *supper of the great God* and the previous one to the *wedding supper of the Lamb*. God is calling the vulturous fowls of heaven to a feast of flesh.

The buzzards will gather, circling with blood-shot eyes and drooling beaks. Yes, God calls them to a great feast...the feast of death. (Ezek. 39:17-20 is very similar, but refers to an earlier battle when the armies of the north first invade Israel.)

(b) The Captains & Kings. *"That ye may eat the flesh of kings...captains...mighty men...horses...the flesh of all men, both free and bond...small and great."*

The Beast and his minions martyred the saints and even turned on the religious harlot (shall make her desolate...and shall eat her flesh 17:16). Now judgment in kind is come, for the Most High God is no respecter of persons! Princes and potentates, captains and kings, warriors and riders, slave and free – all who have lifted a hand against God shall be brought to an ignominious end (Compare the death of Jezebel and Ahab in 1 Kgs. 21:22-26; 22:37-38)

(2) The Conflict (vs. 19) *"...the beast, and the kings of the earth, and their armies, gathered together to make war against him that sat on the horse, and...his army."*

Megiddo will be the final staging area for the armies of the antichrist as he attempts to rally the world to wage war directly against the Lord Jesus and the hosts of heaven. Listen as the antichrist addresses his forces,

"People of the world, we are at war! The time has come for us to unite in a common cause. That which unites us now is far more important than what has divided us before. It is a question of common survival. The time has come for us to take final counsel together against the Lord and His Anointed. He has put Himself in our power. He has dared to appear on earth again. The first time He came, we crucified Him; this time we will destroy Him. We have tried uniting for peace; it has not proved a durable bond. Now let us unite for war! Let us deal with this invasion of our planet once and for all! Let us show these white-robed psalm singers how men, freed of all religious opiates, can fight! Time and again I have given you proofs of my supernatural powers. That dread lord of darkness whom we serve has defied these hosts for countless ages...let us join him in this his inevitable and final victory!" (Adapted from Phillips *Exploring Revelation,* pg. 235)

The phrase ***gathered together***, is in the passive voice (lit. to be gathered). When we refer back to Rev. 16:14-16 we see that though demons will instigate this great military maneuver *(the spirits of devils...go forth...to gather them to the battle...);* ultimately, our sovereign God is in control and He is drawing the enemy to his doom *(of that great day of God Almighty...and He gathered them together into a place called...Armageddon.)*

Also, in Rev. 13:4 we read of the challenge hurled against heaven by the arrogance of idolatrous mankind, *"And they worshipped the dragon who gave power unto the beast: and they worshipped the beast, saying, 'Who is like unto the beast? Who is able to make war with him?'"* Now the world is about to find out who is able (Ps. 2:4)! *"For the great day of his wrath is come; and who shall be able to stand (6:17)?"* Nobody – not even one. How quickly the greatest battle in the history of the world will end!

b. The Judgment of the Beast and False Prophet (vss. 20-21)

(1) The Captives (vs. 20) *"And the beast was taken* [to be arrested, taken into custody; to trap an animal] *and with him the false prophet...These both were cast alive into a lake of fire burning with brimstone.* The outcome of this great conflagration is never in doubt. These are the vanquished foes of a triumphant conquering King!

Once again, we should note Satan's great deceptive powers as expressed here: *"that wrought miracles...with which he deceived them..."*(cf. Mt. 24:5, 11, 24; Rom. 16:18; Eph. 4:14; 5:6; 2 Tim. 3:13; 2 Thes. 2:3; 1 Jn. 3:7; 2 Jn. 7; Rev. 12:9; 13:14; 18:23; 20:3,8,10). Remember, *"an evil and adulterous generation seeketh after a sign."* (Mt. 12:38f).

The two human leaders of the world's rebellion against God are consigned to torment (Dan. 7:11) where they will eventually be joined by those condemned at the final Judgment (20:10-15).

We need to distinguish between the lake of fire and hell (Hades). The unsaved who die before the second coming of

Christ go to Hades (Lk. 16:23). After the White Throne Judgment, death and hell will in turn be cast into the Lake of Fire, the final, eternal place of torment for all the wicked. <u>We know</u> that there is no annihilation in the lake of fire, because the beast and the prophet will still be there after 1,000 years (20:10)! <u>We know</u> that hell is real, that it is a place of conscious, ceaseless agony and a place of darkness and eternal separation from which there is no escape (Lk. 16:23-28; Mt. 8; 12; Jude 13).

(2) The Conquest (vs. 21)

It is worthwhile to note that three times in this chapter Jesus is described as riding on a horse (19:11, 19, 21). It is as if the Holy spirit intends to leave no room for doubt about the literal, physical, visible return of Jesus Christ, when one little word shall fell them – *the remnant were slain with the sword...out of his mouth*(cf. Jn. 18:6)!

Notice the phrase, and *all the fowls were filled with their flesh.* None of the buzzards will go hungry on that day. Oh the irony of Divine retribution (18:5-8)! The kings of the earth drank their fill of fornication (17:2; 18:3). The Beast and the Harlot filled their cups with abominations (17:4) and the blood of the saints (17:6). Now the carrion (cf. 18:2b) are gorged with their rotting corpses.

Church Age	Tribulation	Millennium	Eternity
about 2000 years	7 years	1000 years	Time will be no more
Holy Spirit at Pentecost begins Church Age	Rise of Antichrist and false prophets	Satan bound	New heaven and new earth
The work of God on earth	Revival of Roman Empire	Christ rules	Eternal bliss and joy for those in heaven
preaching the Gospel	Rebuilding of Jewish temple	peace joy no sickness protection holiness healing justice	Eternal suffering and torment for those in hell
saving souls strengthening saints	Russian invasion of Israel		
The work of Satan on earth	Worldwide persecution	Satan loosed	
persecution apostasy confusion sin	Judgments from God	confusion deception	
	Battle of Armageddon	Satan destroyed along with his followers	
	Return of Jesus Christ		

Rapture

Second Coming

F. Vision of Final Things (20:1-22:5)

It will prove helpful at this point to review the outline and *"countdown to eternity"* on pages 182-183. The two final chapters of Revelation deal with John's vision of final events in God's sovereign action leading to the glorious eternal estate of all the redeemed.

1. Satan's Binding for 1,000 Years (20:1-3)

a. He is Shackled with a Great Chain (vss. 1-2) John sees an angel (probably the same as in 9:1, though thought by some to be Michael the Archangel who, according to Rev. 12:7-9, will cast Satan out of heaven during the Tribulation – see notes page 105*) "having a key to the bottomless pit and a great chain in his hand."*

This "bottomless pit" (Rev. 9:1-2, 11; 11:7-8) is also called "the deep" in Luke 8:31 and Rom. 10:7. The literal rendering is "abyss", which may well be a reference to hell itself. The excellent book, <u>Fast Facts on Bible Prophecy</u>, states, "The bottomless pit is always seen as a holding place for beings whose ultimate, eternal abode will be the Lake of Fire."

"And he laid hold on the dragon, that old serpent (a title dating back to Gen. 3:1), *who is the Devil and Satan, and bound him a thousand years."* This binding or "fastening with chains" will render Satan inactive for the 1,000 year earthly reign of Christ. All the Old Testament passages dealing with Messiah's reign reveal the absence of Satan and his evil influence during this entire period.

b. He is shut Up and Sealed in the Bottomless Pit (vs. 3)

(1) The declaration of his imprisonment (3a) *"And cast him into the bottomless pit, and shut him up, and set a seal upon him…"* Wm. R. Newell says, "He is shut within it – shut in his prison; giving relief to the earth, release from all his deceits!"

(2) The design of his imprisonment (3b) *"…that he should deceive the nations no more till the thousand years should be fulfilled…"* From his deception of Eve in the Garden of Eden (Gen. 3) and lasting through the final Tribulation period, Satan has walked about this earth like a roaring lion seeking whom he may devour (1 Pet. 5:8). The purpose behind his confinement at the beginning of the Millennium is to keep him from leading people astray with his deceptive schemes.

(3) The duration of his imprisonment (3c) *"…and after that he must be loosed a little season."* Only **after** the full 1,000 years will Satan be loosed for a brief time (discussed in verses 7-9). This reign of Christ will be a time of unprecedented peace and safety, **free of Satanic influence**. Neither the Bible nor history supports the teaching that Satan is already bound. This is the view of amillennialism, which spiritualizes all the references to Christ's earthly reign, seeing them as symbolic of heaven. Dr. John Walvoord states, "Opposed to the amillennial interpretation…is the uniform revelation of the new Testament which shows that Satan in the present age is a very active person. If anything, he is more active than in preceding ages and is continuing an unrelenting opposition to all that God purposes to do in the present age."

2. Christ's Reigning for One Thousand Years (20:4-6)

The following is a simplified chart to illustrate the chronological order of events leading to the eternal state:

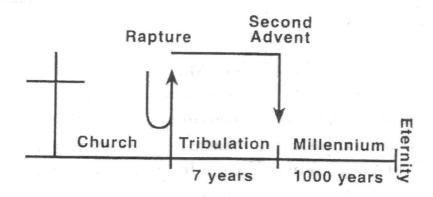

Following His return to earth, Christ will bind Satan (vss. 1-3), judge the nations (Matt. 25) and Israel (Ezek. 20:33-38), all in preparation for His glorious 1,000 year reign (**note** the six-fold reference to "one thousand years" in verses 2-7. This is not a symbolic term, but rather a literal 1,000 years!!!)

       a. Those Who Judge (vs. 4a) "And I saw thrones, and they sat on them, and judgment was given unto them…"

Take a moment to read Isa. 1:26; Matt. 19. 28; Lk. 22:29-30; and 1 Cor. 6:2. From these passages, it appears likely that these judges (not revealed in our Rev. 20:4 passage) include Christ, Who has control of all judgment, and the twenty four elders of Rev. 4:4, 10. We believe the 24 elders to be representative of redeemed Israel (12 tribes) and the Church (12 apostles), both groups of which are involved in the judgment process. The process of judgment here is to determine who is worthy to enter the Kingdom reign of Christ.

b. Those Who Reign (vs. 4b) Those who John sees living and reigning with Christ for 1,000 years are the martyred saints of the Tribulation period. These suffering and martyred believers are clearly depicted in Rev. 7:9-17.

c. Those Who Are Dead (vs. 5a) *"But the rest of the dead lived not again until the thousand years were finished."* This clearly represents the unsaved, whose spirits are imprisoned in hell until the White Throne Judgment of Rev. 20:11-15. Walvoord states, "The resurrection at the end of the Millennium is obviously a bodily resurrection as it includes the unsaved.

d. Those Who Take Part in the First Resurrection (vss. 5b-6) Christ being the "first fruits" of the resurrection (1 Cor. 15:20), this reference to the "first resurrection" relates to all the redeemed, including Old Testament saints, Church Age believers, and those saved during the Tribulation.

Comparing Daniel 12:2 and Rev. 20:14; 21:8, there will be two resurrections of infinitely different character – one of the righteous and one of the unrighteous. As declared here, *"Blessed and holy is he that hath part in the first resurrection; on such the second death hath no power, but they shall be priests of God and of Christ, and shall reign with him a thousand years."*

3. Satan's Loosing & Doom (20:7-10)

Once again, those who deny a literal, physical kingdom rule of Christ on the earth (amillennialism) have difficulty with this text. Their belief that Satan is bound during the present Church Age is in conflict with the clear revelation in verses 7-10 that Satan's binding will occur during Christ's future earthly rule. Verse 3 predicted that Satan would be released from his isolation cell (the "abyss") at the end of Christ's reign – and that's exactly what occurs.

a. Satan's Loosing (vss. 7-9)

(1) From His Prison – The Abyss. *"And when the thousand years are expired, Satan shall be loosed out of his prison."* The climax of the Millennial rule of our Lord will begin with Satan's release from the Bottomless Pit (20:1). Why will God release him? Here God's final test of man demonstrates the total corruption of the human heart! Even in perfect environment (where the lion lays down with the lamb), even with perfect justice in government (Christ will be the King), and even with the elimination of disease and poverty (man's life span will extend for a thousand years as in the pre-flood earth), even with all of this, men will still reject the love of God in Christ. Such stubborn rebellion will demonstrate once and for all that mankind's problem is sin…not the environment, not political or economic inequality…just sin (Mt. 15:19; Rom. 3:10-23).

(2) For His Purpose – To Deceive. *"And shall go out to deceive the nations…to gather them together to battle…"* Phillips writes, "Throughout the Millennium, righteousness has reigned…but, as the ages come and go, countless are born…with sinful natures, needing to be saved, just as today. Children born of believing parents today sometimes become gospel-hardened; so, during the Millennium many will become glory-hardened. They will submit to Christ's rule…[but] many will render only feigned obedience…Sin will reign secret in their hearts…The devil will find fertile soil in their souls [when he is released]. Retreating…as far as possible from the central glory, the disaffected…will begin to congregate. They are called, "Gog and Magog" in the text…The memory of Russia's disaster [during the Tribulation, Ezek. 38-39] will linger on, and Gog and Magog will lend their names symbolically to the dissidents of earth. Satan will seek them out and find them only too willing to listen to his lies. They will rejoice at his bold claims, flock to his standards, and follow him headlong into rebellion." (_Exploring Revelation_, pg. 240)

The multitudes that follow Satan in this final rebellion against Christ's throne are described as "Gog and Magog." At first glance, many confuse this with the prophecy in Ezekiel 38-39. But several factors help us distinguish the two. The war in Ezekiel speaks of an invasion of Israel by Russia and a few allies, whom God will miraculously destroy far north of Jerusalem. In _this_ passage, the enemies come from the "four quarter of the earth" and encompass Jerusalem before being destroyed. In Ezek. 38, 39, although fire is _part_ of God's judgment (39:6), it takes seven months to bury the dead (39:12). In _this_ battle the enemy's bodies will be **_devoured_** (lit. "To consume completely") by fire. Though these two battles seem to differ in several respects, their ultimate purpose is the same – Satan leading men in war against God! In Rev. 20, Satan's purpose is to destroy the seat of Christ's authority ("the beloved city" of Jerusalem) and ascend the throne himself. But all of his efforts are doomed to fail.

b. Satan's Doom (vs. 10)

(1) Cast into the lake of Fire "**_And the devil that deceived them was cast into the lake of fire and brimstone…_**" Not only is Satan's army of rebellion destroyed by fire from heaven, but his final destiny will be hell-fire! While unsaved humanity will be raised to face Christ's judgment (vss. 11-15), Satan will be instantly consigned to the "lake of fire," where the Antichrist and False Prophet have been for a thousand years (19:20). No RSVP will be necessary... this has been his destiny since his revolt against God in eternity past (Mt. 25:41). Jesus also has a place prepared for the believer (John 14:2,3); but what a difference there will be!

The Greek word, *gehenna,* is usually translated "hell" (Mt. 5: 22, 29-30; 10:28; 18:9; 23:15,33; Mk. 9:43-47; Lk. 12:5; Jam. 3:6). There is no contextual, grammatical or hermeneutical basis for a non-literal interpretation here! HELL IS REAL!

Notes on the Bible's Teaching about Hell

Liberal theologians, rejecting the clear teaching of the Bible, have long ridiculed the very idea of a literal hell. Yet, the Lord Jesus Christ spoke of hell 19 times in the Gospels – more than He mentioned heaven. To deny one is to deny the other! Sadly, today's religious polls reveal that fewer and fewer professing Christians and main-line denominational churches no long believe in the existence of hell (in 1990, only 50% of Baptists, 10% of Episcopalians, 10% of Methodists, and 15% of Presbyterians). This is a sad commentary on the church's view of the authority and inspiration of the Bible. How we need to get back to the Book!

1. *Hell is a Literal Place* – Jesus believed this and taught it with urgency (Mt. 11:23; 16:18; Lk. 16:22-23; Rev. 1:18).

2. *Hell is a Place of Unspeakable Suffering* – Mk. 9:44 describes it as "the fire that never shall be quenched, where their worm dieth not…" (cf. Mt. 8:12; 25:41; Lk. 13:23-28; Jude 13).

    a. Effects on Speech – Total silence (except for weeping and gnashing of teeth)! 1 Sam. 2:9 says, "the wicked shall be silent in darkness."

    b. Effects on Sight – Total Darkness! Ps. 44:9 reads, "…they shall never see light."

    c. Effects on Touch – Total Helplessness! "Bind him hand and foot…cast him into out darkness."

3. *Hell was not Prepared for Man* – Mt. 25:41 reveals that hell was designed for the judgment of Satan and the fallen angels (cf. Rev. 20:10; Jude 6-7).

4. *Hell is the Final Destiny of the Unsaved* – All men who reject the salvation work of the Lord Jesus Christ on the cross will be judged by their own works and will be condemned in hell (Rev. 20:11f).

5. *Hell Translates Three Different Greek Words* -

    a. ***Sheol*** – (used 65 times in the Bible, 31 times translated "hell") – usually referring to the grave or the place of those who have departed from this life, whether righteous or wicked (Ps. 16:10; 30:3; Job 24:19; Ps. 9:17).

b. *Hades* – a NT word similar to Sheol in usage but more often emphasizes the suffering of the unrighteous dead (Mt. 11:23; 16:18; Lk. 10:15; 16:23; Acts 11:27, 31; 1 Cor. 15:55; Rev. 1:18; 6:8; 20:13-14).

c. *Gehenna* – The valley of Hinnom was the place where Jewish apostasy reached its zenith in the worship of Molech (1Kings 11:7) and which Josiah converted into a public incinerator (2 Kgs. 23:13,14). This abominable place of continual burning became a fitting description of hell (Mt. 5:22; Mk. 9:43; Lk. 12:5; Rev. 20:10

(2) Confined Forever and Ever- *"…and shall be tormented day and night for ever and ever."* This "lake of fire" is a definite place of eternal punishment for those who reject Christ. There they will suffer physically and spiritually along with the fallen angels. Apparently this horrible place will be a body of super-heated fluid fire.

NOTE: God *is not willing that any should perish, but that all should come to repentance* (2 Pt. 3:9). No one need go to hell. The way of escape was provided at the cross 2000 years ago. *For whosoever shall call upon the name of the Lord shall be saved* (Rom. 10:13). Trust in Jesus Christ today!

4. The Great White Throne Judgment (20:11-15)

a. The Throne (vs. 11) – *"And I saw a great white throne, and him that sat on it, from whose face the earth and the heaven fled away…"(*cf. Rev. 6:17). Mankind should never forget that there will be a reckoning with Almighty God. This passage portrays God's final dealings with sinful man. Even the earth will be judged/cleansed (2 Pt. 3:10-12) in preparation for the new heaven and new earth (Rev. 21:1).

(1) Why is it Great? *Because* Almighty Power from the infinite God of Justice will be executed. *Because* every lost person from Cain to Antichrist will be there. *Because* of the awesome consequences of the judgment.

(2) Why is it White? *Because* of the infinite purity and holiness of the Judge and the contrast with man's wickedness. Jesus will be the Judge (Jn. 5:22; Acts 10:42), perfect justice the result.

b. The Judgment (vss. 12-15)

(1) The Books Opened (vs.12) *"And I saw the dead, small and great stand before God..."* God is no respecter of persons (Dan. 12:2; Heb. 9:27). Two sets of books are opened: *the book of life* (the roll call of the saved) and *the books* [plural] which record the "works" of the unsaved. These works will be the basis of man's condemnation, for they are no substitute for the blood of Christ (Rom. 2:5-6)!

(2) The Sea & Hell Opened (vs. 13) All the dead will be gathered from their graves and from Hades to hear the Divine Verdict pronounced and to face the final judgment. God's great enemies are forever defeated (1 Cor. 15:26).

(3) The Lake of Fire Filled (vss. 14-15) *"And whosoever was not found written in the book of life was cast into the lake of fire."* To reject the gospel of Jesus Christ is to embrace eternal condemnation. There will be no second chances there.

5. The Eternal State of the Redeemed (21:1-22:5)

This is the final section under John's Vision of Final Things (20:1-22:5), where God reveals Satan's binding during the millennium (20:1-3); Christ's reigning for 1,000 years (20:4-6); Satan's brief loosing (20:7-10); and the final White Throne judgment of all the unsaved (20:11-15).

In these verses leading up to the grand conclusion of 22:6-21 the glorious New Jerusalem is declared, described and characterized.

a. The New City Declared (21:1-8)

(1) What John Sees (vss. 1-2)

(a) "And I saw a new heaven and a new earth; for the first heaven and the first earth were passed; and there was no more sea."

An interesting artist's concept of the various phases through which the earth has passed, leading to the Divinely created New Heavens and New Earth, is shown below. In light of the fact that the present earth is more than 2/3 water, it is fascinating that the only body of water spoken of in the new earth is the *"pure river of water of life"* in Revelation 22:1! Ryrie comments, "Whatever else this phrase may mean, it seems to indicate the end of the old order (Exodus 20:11). As understood literally this indicates a complete change in climatic conditions."

In conjunction with the destruction of the old heavens and earth, and the creation of new heavens and earth, take a moment to read Isaiah 65:17-20 and 2 Peter 3:4-14.

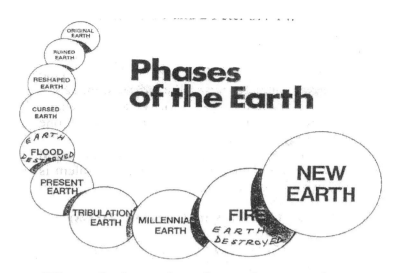

Phases of the Earth

ORIGINAL EARTH

RUINED EARTH

RESHAPED EARTH

CURSED EARTH

EARTH FLOOD DESTROYED

PRESENT EARTH

TRIBULATION EARTH

MILLENNIAL EARTH

FIRE EARTH DESTROYED

NEW EARTH

When God speaks of creating _new_ heavens and _new_ earth, He is not referring to a mere cleansing of the earth or a refurbishing of the old earth! The word "create" in Isaiah 65:17 as relates to the new heavens and new earth is **bara** in Hebrew, the same word used of the original creation in Genesis 1 meaning to make out of nothing, the Divine calling into being of that which had no previous existence (in the Latin language, **ex nihilo**, "out of nothing".

(b) *"And I John saw the holy city, the New Jerusalem, coming down out of heaven, prepared as a bride adorned for her husband."* (Compare Heb. 11:10; 12:22-24; Rev. 3:12; 21:10-27) here is the eternal dwelling place for all the saved of all ages. Since Israel, an earthly people with earthly promises, will live eternally on the new earth, we agree with Dr. Walvoord, who states in his commentary on Revelation, "...the New Jerusalem is withdrawn from the earthly scene in connection with the destruction of the old earth, and later comes down to the new earth." Thus, as illustrated in the following diagram, we Church Age believers, who have a heavenly inheritance, will dwell for eternity with those saved people who had an earthly inheritance.

Comparing verse 2 with Hebrews 11:10, F.W. Grant, in his commentary, states: "Why should it not be the bride city, named from the bride-*church*, whose home it is, and yet contains other occupants?...the heavenly city, the dwelling place of God, permitting none of the redeemed to be outside it, but opening it's gates widely to all."

(2) What John Hears (vss. 3-8)
(a) He hears the promise of a new community (vss. 3-4) In this glorious eternal state God will dwell with us and deliver us from all former limitations:
- **God dwells with His people (vs. 3)** *"...Behold, the tabernacle of God is with men, and He will dwell with them...and be their God."* By contrast, He dwelt with his Old Testament people in the wilderness Tabernacle (Ex. 25:8; 40:34-38); He dwells with His own today, our bodies being His dwelling place (1 Cor. 3:16; 6:19); but the greatest realization by far is that for all eternity, He will dwell intimately with all His own!

- **God delivers his people from all former limitations (vs. 4)** *"And God shall wipe away all tears from their eyes; and there shall be no more death, neither sorrow, nor crying, neither shall there be any more pain; for the former things are passed away."* GLORY! All the hurtful associations belonging to this earthly existence will "BE NO MORE" ...a guaranteed future certainty!

(b) He hears the proclamation of a new constitution (vss. 5-8)
- **This new constitution guarantees Almighty God to be a faithful Father to all the saved (vs. 5-7)** *"And He that*

sat upon the throne said, Behold, I make all things new..." 1 Cor. 15:20-28 declares that Christ, having put down all rule, authority, and power through His resurrection, will ultimately "deliver up the kingdom to God, even the Father", Who will make all things new – a drastic change from the old order! Indeed, everything the Father commands is to be declared *"faithful and true".* In verse 6 the One Who *is "Alpha and Omega, the beginning and the end"* promises to give all who thirst *"of the fountain of the water of life"* the final answer to Psalm 42:1-2 and John 7:37-38! *"He that overcometh"* in verse 7 is positional overcoming, achieved only through faith in Christ.

• **This new constitution guarantees Almighty God to be a fearsome Foe to all the unsaved, who** *"shall have their part in the lake which burneth with fire and brimstone, which is the second death."* (compare Mk. 9:49; Rev. 21:27)

b. The New City Described (21:9-21) John is now afforded the privilege of beholding the New Jerusalem in intricate detail. As the Jerusalem of old was called *"The Holy City," so will the new (21:2). Our eternal abode will be a Holy City! Anderson Scott wrote, "A city is the first ambition and then despair of man...Men are proud of a city; they name themselves by its name; they sun themselves in its power and splendor, and yet in the hands of men, the city has become a monster which devours its children."* Not so in the New Jerusalem! This city will be the fulfillment of all the hopes and aspirations of man for tranquility, peace, joy and glory. Because...

(1) It Has the Glory of God (vss. 9-11)

(a) Revealing the Lamb's Wife (vs. 9) *"Come here, I will shew thee the bride, the Lamb's wife".* The city is clearly identified as the Bride of Christ (vss. 2, 9), the eternal home of the Church which He has been preparing for 2000 years (Jn. 14:2)!

(b) Revealing the Great City (vss. 10-11) *"And he carried me away...and shewed me that great city, the holy Jerusalem, descending out of heaven from God."* This wonderful city is seen descending out of heaven and suspended in the heavens, illuminating the new earth with the glory of God (vss. 3, 10). What would have seemed absolutely fantastic to John in his day is comprehensible and even possible in our day. But no modern space station is even worthy to be compared with the future magnificence of the Eternal City of God!

This city is "great" for two reasons: Christ has prepared it and it will reflect His undiminished glory (cf. 22:5). The city's light will be the radiance of His presence [the Shekinah Glory will be in our midst!] and is described in terms of the brilliant hues and reflections of the precious gemstones. As the old hymn says, "But a blessed day is coming, when His glory shall be seen."

(2) It Has a Great Wall and Gates (vss. 12-14)
(a) Its Gates (vss. 12-13) Twelve gates with twelve inscriptions, protected by twelve angels – apparently honor guards (like America's Old Guard" that keep watch over Arlington's Tomb of the Unknown Soldier). Each gate is engraved with a tribe of Israel, three on each side of the city, just as they camped in order during the Exodus. (cf. Ezek. 48:31f)
(b) Its Wall (vs. 14) In vs. 12 the wall is said to be "great and high," symbolizing the absolute security we will enjoy and the absolute exclusion of the unsaved. The foundation stones of the city wall are engraved as memorials to the twelve apostles. Note: even in eternity, Israel and the

Church are distinguished by God, although both are part of His redeemed people.

That there are three gates on each side of the city (vs. 13) reveals the wonderful freedom of movement and access that will be ours. No visa or passport will be required – other than the blood of Christ! *Have you been washed in the blood?*

(3) It has Specific Dimensions (vss. 15-17) The *reed* was a common measuring instrument, nearly 11' long (six times a cubit, plus six handbreadths, Ez. 40:5; 42:15). The city itself will be a cube (or a pyramid), 1400 miles square and tall (1 furlong/stadia = approx. 606'). The cube was considered by the ancient Greeks to be a symbol of perfection. Ryrie observes in his commentary that "the foursquare shape of the city, reminds us of the fourfold dimensions of the love of God in Eph. 3:18."

The cubit (vs. 17) is measured from the elbow to the end of the middle finger (approx. 18"). Imagine a city that stretched from Wilmington to Memphis, and from New York City to Miami – that is how massive the New Jerusalem will be!

(4) It Has Glorious Beauty (vss. 18-21)
(a) The Beauty of the Wall (vss. 18-20) The importance of the precious stones (cf. Ex. 28:17f) mentioned is not their monetary value, but their matchless beauty and variety reflecting the beauty of God's holiness and glory (jasper – green; sapphire – blue; chalcedony – green; emerald – green; sardonyx – brown/white; sardius – red; chrysolyte – yellow; beryl – green; topaz – yellow; chrysoprase – apple green; jacinth – blue; amethyst – purple.

(b) The Beauty of the Gates (vs. 21) Imagine pearls of this size! Phillips writes, "How appropriate…a pearl is a gem formed within the oyster – the only one formed by living flesh. The humble oyster receives an irritation or a wound, and around the offending article that has penetrated and hurt it, the oyster builds a pearl. The pearl, we might say, is the answer of the oyster to that which injured it. The glory land is God's answer, in Christ, to wicked men who crucified heaven's beloved and put Him to open shame. How like God it is to make the gates of the New Jerusalem of pearl. The saints as they come and go will be forever reminded, as they pass the gates of glory that access to God's home is only because of Calvary. Think of the size of those gates! Think of the supernatural pearls from which they are made! Those pearls, hung eternally at the access routes to glory, will remind us forever of One who hung upon a tree."

And the streets of the city were pure gold, as it were transparent glass (vs. 21b). Translucent gold, crystal clear in color – it will take our breath away!

Streets of Gold
The Streets of Heaven are paved with Gold.
But, not with heavy metal gold, as others think.
More like golden leaves, fallen from September trees.
Like glistening sidewalks, covered after autumn rains.
As I walk with God each day, such beauty fills my soul in praise.
A vision of what I'll someday see, when God call, "Come home!" to me.

c. The New City Distinguished (21:22-22:5)
(1) It Has No Earthly Temple – *The Lord God Almighty and the Lamb are the temple of it (vs. 22)*

(2) Its Source of Light is – the glory of God and the Lamb (vs. 23)

(3) Its Occupants are – the nations of those who are saved (vss. 24, 26)

(4) Its Gates are Always Open and – there shall be no night (vs.25)

(5) Its Inhabitants will be only – they who are written in the Lamb's Book of Life (vs. 27)

(6) It will have *"a pure river of water of life…proceeding out of the throne of God and of the Lamb"* **(22:1)** Just as man enjoys water and, indeed, cannot live without it in this life, God will provide a refreshing and abundant and life-perpetuating river in the eternal state. And not to go unnoticed: Our Lord Jesus, the very Lamb of God, will still be on the throne in the eternal state!

Walvoord makes an interesting correlation, stating that "This river corresponds to the present believer's experience of the outflow of the Spirit and eternal life." His reference is to John 7:38-39, where "Jesus stood and cried out, saying, If any man thirst, let him come unto Me and drink. He that believeth on Me, as the Scripture hath said, out of his heart shall flow rivers of living water. But this spoke he of the Spirit, Whom they that believe on Him should receive…" HALLELUJAH! We don't have to look to the future to experience "rivers of living water"!

(7) It will have *"the tree of life…in the midst of the street and on either side of the river"* **(22:5).** The picture given here is that the river of life will flow through the middle of the city, the tree of life actually spanning the river.

As a reminder, this tree of life was in the original Garden of Eden, along with the tree of the knowledge of good and evil (Gen. 2:9). God had to drive man out of this Garden (Gen. 3:22-24); lest he eat of this tree of life and live forever (this would have nullified the Divine sentence of death declared in 2:17.

(a) This tree of life will provide perpetual fruit. What a glorious and eternal "fruit of the month club" this will be! Truly, God cares for His own in every way! Compare this same tree of life with that in the Garden of Eden in Genesis 3:22-24.

(b) This tree of life will promote perpetual health, as *"the leaves of the tree are for the health* (not "healing" as in the English text) *of the nations."* The purpose is not to provide healing (we already have that in the eternal state) but rather to promote for all eternity a vibrant, pure, powerful, and healthy life – ALL PRAISE TO OUR SAVIOR!

(8) It will include the service of the saints before God's throne (22:3). The curse of sin, once-for-all removed by the blood of the sacrificial Lamb of God (Christ), will have no more harmful effects on those in Christ! Our service will then be perfectly unhindered and effective.

(9) It will provide immediate access to God's presence and glory, since His servants "shall see His face". (22:4a) Here is final proof of the complete consecration of God's servants to His service. Oh, that we, through total yieldedness, would enjoy something of His presence and glory today!

(10) It will assure eternal Divine ownership, since *"His name shall be in their foreheads."* **(22:4b)** In our present incomplete state it is

all too easy to forget that "we are not our own, having been bought with the precious blood of Jesus" (1 Cor. 6:19) But in the eternal state there will be question as to Who owns us. Take a moment to compare Rev. 3:12; 7:3; and 14:1. Walvoord comments: "The fact that they shall see His face demonstrates beyond question that these are glorified saints (1 John 3:2)." And the best part is that the reference is to those of us who have received Christ for salvation in this life!

(11) It will be conducive to the eternal reign of the redeemed (22:5) *"And there shall be no night there; and they need no lamp, neither light of the sun; for the Lord God giveth them light, and they shall reign forever and ever."*

In his commentary on Revelation Tim LaHaye makes a fitting comment: "Today we are dependent on the sun for light and heat, changing our apparel or place of residence or habits of agriculture in accordance with the cycle of the sun. At that time we will not be limited to external objects, for God Himself will provide a consistent pattern of light that is ideally suited to us."

Just as Christ, the King of kings and Lord of lords, will reign on this old earth in the Millennial Kingdom and in the New Heavens and New Earth in the eternal state, so we are promised the privilege of reigning with Him.

To believers who have had to suffer for their faith in Christ, it is reassuring to know that the Bible never discusses our eternal abode theoretically. God's reflections on this glorious place prepared for the redeemed is always intensely practical and comforting. Dr. Louis Talbot said, "Reflections on heaven are never a waste of time. Rather they provide a moral force for our practical life upon this earth. A true believer, longing for glory, is never too heavenly minded to be of no earthly use."

A FEW BIBLICAL REALITIES
Of OUR ETERNAL HOME

1. Our eternity will be a life of unending fellowship with our great triune God (John 14:1-3; Rev. 21:3)
2. Our eternity will be a life of unending rest (Job 3:17; Rev. 14:13)
3. Our eternity will be a life of perfect and unending holiness (Rev. 21:27)
4. Our eternity will be a life of full and unending knowledge (1 Cor. 13:12; Eph. 4:13)
5. Our eternity will be a life of freedom from pain accompanied by unending joy (Jude 24; Rev. 21:4)
6. Our eternity will be a life of unbroken fellowship and companionship with all the redeemed of all ages (1 Thess. 4:17; Rev. 5:9-13)
7. Our eternity will be a life of unhindered and unending service (Rev. 22:3)
8. Our eternity will be a life of exceeding and unending glory (Rom. 8:18; 2 Cor. 4:17; Col. 3:4)
9. Our eternity will be a life of continual worship and ascribing of blessing and honor and glory upon our glorious God. (Rev. 7:9-12; 19:1-6)

The Conclusion of God's Word (22:6-21)

Now we come to the epilogue of the book and the end of God's written revelation to man. This final portion includes both words of comfort and words of caution. An angel (vss. 6, 8-11), Christ Himself (vss. 7, 12-16, 20), the Holy Spirit (vss. 17-19), and the ages Apostle John (vs. 21) confirm all that is recorded in the Apocalypse.

A. The Faithful & True Word of God (22:6-11)

Not only is the Living Word (Jesus) declared to be faithful and true (Jn. 1:14, 17; 14:6; 1 Cor. 1:9; 10:13; 1 Thes. 5:24; 2 Thes. 3:3; Rev. 1:5; 3:14), but so also is the Written Word (the Bible) (Ps. 19:9; Ps. 119:86, 138; 1 Thes. 1:15; 1 Tim. 4:9; 2 Tim. 2:15; Rev. 21:5).

1. The Bible's Accuracy (vs. 6) *These sayings are...*
a. *Faithful* – speaks of the characteristic of a person or thing that can be relied upon or is trustworthy. One thing you and I can count on, everything written in Revelation will eventually be literally fulfilled!

b. *True* – as opposed to what is feigned or false. The bible is free from error and is totally reliable.

c. *...of the Holy prophets* – as opposed to all false prophets (1 Kgs. 18:20f). The test of Biblical prophets and prophecy is 100% accuracy, with no margin of error!

d. *sent [to be shown]...things which must shortly come to pass.* – Again, the purpose of this book is to reveal Christ and His plan for future events (Rev. 1:1).

2. The Bible's Authority (vss. 7-9)

Here we have the first of three final assurances of Christ's return (22:7, 12, 20). The book opened with the words, "Behold, He cometh" (1:7), and it concludes with Christ's promise that, "Surely I come quickly." The word "quickly" means that when our Lord comes for His own, it will be with lightning-like speed (1 Cor. 15:52). The suddenness of His coming will catch many unawares (Strauss, <u>Revelation</u>, pg. 361).

Blessed is he that keepeth…also reminds the reader of the opening promise of the book (1:3). To *keep* means to guard, watch over, or to preserve the Word of God. This is the duty of every child of God. Christ's imminent return serves as a present impetus for holy living and as a blessed hope for the future!

I John saw these things and heard them…John adds his personal confirmation, of the accuracy and authority of the Word of God, to that of the Lord, the prophets, and the angels (cf. 1 Jn. 1:1-4). John's prostrate posture is an involuntary response of a sinful man before an angel of glory who reflects the holiness of God (1:17; 5:8, 14; 7:11; 11:16; 19:10). Yet, he is reminded once again that only God is worthy of worship (vs. 9).

3. The Bible's Accessibility (vss. 10-11)

Seal not the sayings of the prophecy of this book…(cf. 1:1-3; Dan. 12:9). Revelation ("unveiling") is intended to be read and understood, especially *since the time is at hand* (Jam. 5:8; 1 Pt. 4:7). To shy away from it or fail to teach it is to grieve the blessed Holy Spirit who inspired it and illumines it for us.

When the time for Christ's return does arrive, the final destiny of sinners and saints (believers) will be settled forever (vs. 11). There will be no second chances for those who put off receiving Christ.

B. The Final Testimony of Jesus Christ (22:12-16)

The last words of any man are given great weight, even in a court of law. Here we have the last recorded words of Jesus Christ to His Bride. We would do well to give heed to them.

1. I Am Coming Again (vs. 12)

"And, behold...and my reward is with me to give every man according as his work shall be." The promise of Jesus coming in vs. 7 was related to our obligation to obey the Word. This time it is related to stewardship and rewards. Our salvation, sanctification and glorification are all works of the grace of God on our behalf, but there are rewards for faithful service (1 Cor. 3:11-15). Even these will all be grace, since it is the Holy Spirit that enables our service for God!

Woe to any man who rejects the work of Christ on the cross and attempts to stand before God's judgment on the basis of his own righteousness (Isa. 64:6; Eph. 2:8,9; Tit. 3:5; Rev. 20:11-15).

2. I Am the Final answer (vss. 13-15)

These glorious titles of Jesus Christ, by which He identifies Himself in vs. 13, once again take us back to the beginning of the book (cf. 1:8, 17; 2:8). For a worthwhile devotional study, scan this book for every title used of Christ and you will be amazed at what is revealed about His person and His work!

*"**Blessed are they that do his commandments that they may have right to the tree of life...and enter in**"*. Verse 14 is the last of the seven beatitudes found in Revelation (1:3; 14:13; 16:15; 19:9; 20:6; 22:7). Do not misunderstand; Jesus is not saying that we are saved by keeping the law. In John's Gospel (6:29) we read, *"**This is the work of God, that you believe on him whom he has sent**"*. Later, John refers to believers as those who "keep his commandments" rather than practicing sin as a pattern of life (1 Jn. 2:3-11).

In contrast with our access to the Kingdom, the wicked will be excluded. According to vs. 15, those who practice idolatry and immorality (cf. Rev. 9:21; 18:23) will find the gates of heaven posted with the following sign:

NO TRESPASSING!

But outside are the dogs and sorcerers and sexually immoral and murderers and idolaters, and whoever loves and practices a lie. (22:15)

The word "without/outside" might sound like it refers to those outside the New Jerusalem but still on the New Earth. Not so! The Lord is speaking of those who are entirely outside His Kingdom:

- There will be no sinners in the eternal kingdom.
- Rev. 21:27 says that only those whose names are in the Book of Life will enter the eternal Kingdom.
- Rev. 21:8 makes it clear that the wicked will be condemned in the Lake of Fire forever.

---

3. I Am the Fulfillment of All Prophecy (vs. 16)

"I am the root and the offspring of David, and the bright and morning star." Isaiah 11:1, 10; Numbers 24:17 and Zechariah 6:12 make plain that these names were Messianic titles. Jesus is clearly declaring one final time, to all who will listen, "I am the Messiah of Israel, the Savior of the World." He is the fulfillment of all Biblical prophecy and the Final Answer to the desperate needs of sinful mankind.

C. The Final Testimony of the Holy Spirit (22:17-21)

1. The Last Welcome – *A Plea* (vs. 17)

Here is the Spirit of God's final plea for men to turn to Jesus Christ. 2 Cor. 6:2 tells us that "Now is the accepted time, now is the day of salvation!" Rev. 1:3 says, "The time is at hand." My friend, how long will you wait? God does not promise us tomorrow! If you reject the final testimony of God there is no hope for you (Mk. 3:29).

a. The Spirit's Invitation – *"Come!"*

All three times in this verse the word "Come!" is a present imperative (a repetitive command). The Holy Spirit is extending a worldwide, inclusive opportunity for salvation by grace through faith in the Lord Jesus Christ (Jn. 3:16). He is not willing that any should perish (2 Pt. 3:9), and issues this final call (Jn. 16:8).

b. The Spirit's Expectation – *Say, "Come!"*

Here I see the worldwide responsibility of the Church, acting in concert with the Spirit of God, to deliver this invitation to all men, everywhere (Mt. 28:18-20). The old hymn captures the meaning:

"You have heard the joyful sound,

Jesus saves! Jesus saves!

Spread the tidings all around,

Jesus saves! Jesus saves!"

c. The Soul in Desperation – *"Come!"*

Salvation is freely offered to anyone who will humbly cry out to God for mercy (Isa. 55:1-3; Jn. 4:10-15, 30; Mt. 11:28). Ya'll Come, Hear!

The Holy Spirit Revealed in Revelation

The Doctrine of the Triune Godhead is clearly revealed in the Apocalypse. *Grace to you and peace from Him who is, and who was, and who is to come* (God the Father); *and from the seven spirits* (The fullness of God the Holy Spirit) *which are before His throne; and from Jesus Christ* (God the Son) (1:4).

In John's prophecy there are at least 18 references to the Holy Spirit:

- In the Letters to the Seven Churches (Rev. 2-3), each church is challenged to give heed to the Spirit of God, "he that hath an ear to hear, let him hear what the Spirit say..." (2:7, 11, 17, 29; 3:6, 13, 22).
- The phrase, "the seven spirits" occurs four times (1:4; 3:1; 4:5; 5:6) and speaks of the seven-fold fullness of the ministry of the Holy Spirit (Isa. 11:2).
- The Spirit was active in the life and experience of John, [*I was in the Spirit on the Lords' day...*" (1:10; 4:2; 17:3; 21:10)] Just as He is still actively involved in every believer's life today!
- It is the Spirit of God who woos the unbeliever to Christ and offers the Final Call to the Unsaved to come to Christ for Salvation (22:17).

2. The Last Warning – *A Promise* (vss. 18-19)

God not only promises blessings for those who read and keep this book, He also promises severe judgment for those that trifle with its sacred contents. What is the bottom line? Don't tamper with the Word of God!

a. Beware Additions (vs. 18)

The Latter Day Saints have erred in this regard with the Book of Mormon, which is actually titled, "Another Testament of Jesus Christ" (read Gal. 1:6-10). Others have erred by adding the Apocryphal books to the canon of Scripture. The Watchtower society (Jehovah's Witnesses) adds to the text of John 1:1 in an attempt to bolster their false teaching denying the Deity of Jesus Christ.

b. Beware Deletions (vs.19)

I personally don't recommend the Readers' Digest version of the Bible! Critical scholars have always deleted anything and everything from the Word of God that troubles their conscience or goes against their pre-conceived ideas about Jesus. How foolhardy is the pride of man.

3. The Last Word – *A Prayer* (vss. 20-21)

a. Jesus' Lasting Assurance (vs. 20)

More prophecy speaks of Christ's 2nd advent than of His incarnation. Just as the 1st advent is undeniable history, even more so the 2nd. Biblical prophecy is not mere speculation, nor is it sensationalism. It is certain-sure, future history pre-viewed for us by the Holy Spirit. Revelation reads like the latest headline news!

Coming Soon!

To the Heavens above You...

The Lord Jesus Christ, King of Glory!

The question is, "Are you ready?" Ready or not, He is coming again...and very soon indeed!

b. John's Last Amen (vs. 21)

"Amen. Even so, come, Lord Jesus. The grace of our Lord Jesus Christ be with you all. Amen". Amen is used in Hebrew and Greek to affirm the trustworthiness of a state-ment, to declare it faithful and true. Sometimes it is translated, "verily" and at other, "most assuredly." John uses it over 25 times in his gospel! Today we might say, "That settles it!"

John's appeal for Jesus Christ's return is an almost involuntary prayer...the earnest cry that ought to fill every believer's heart – every day and every night. Are you longing for Jesus to come for His Bride? Are you living in the light of His soon appearing? I hope so, dear friend, because He is coming back. Why, I can almost hear the trumpet sounding now! Until that day, hold on to His Grace!

A Celebration of Victory

Ten thousand times ten thousand
In sparkling raiment bright,
The armies of the ransomed saints
Throng up the steeps of light:
'Tis finished, all is finished,
Their light with death and sin;
Fling open wide the golden gates,
And let the victors in.

What rush of hallelujahs
Fills all the earth and sky!
What ringing of a thousand harps
Bespeaks the triumph nigh!
O day for which creation
And all its tribes were made!

O joy, for all its former woes
A thousand-fold repaid.

Dean Alford

About the Author

Dr. Ralph Richardson graduated from high school in Miami, Florida; attended John B. Stetson University and earned an A.B. degree from Wheaton College, Th. M. degree from Dallas Theological Seminary, and D. Min. degree from Luther Rice Seminary.

Dr. Richardson was Founder and former pastor of Church of the Open Door, Fayetteville, NC from 1969-1982. President of Carolina Bible College, Fayetteville, NC. 1979-1997.
Chancellor of Carolina Bible College, Fayetteville, NC. 1997-present.
He is currently President of Bible Alive Ministries, Inc. conducting luncheon Bible studies in various areas, correspondence home studies, radio Bible teaching, Bible conferences in local churches, and pulpit supply on request.
Other books by Dr. Richardson are:
"Bible Digest – A Brief Guide to Every Book of the Bible" and "Major Doctrines of the Christian Faith".
His wife Bertelle served as Registrar at Carolina Bible College; 1979-1997. She is a Bible teacher, author, artist and homemaker. They have two children and one grandson.

NOTES

72014945R00116

Made in the USA
Columbia, SC
13 June 2017